Performance Results
in
Value Added Reporting

Performance Results
in
Value Added Reporting

AHMED RIAHI-BELKAOUI

QUORUM BOOKS
Westport, Connecticut • London

657
R48p

Library of Congress Cataloging-in-Publication Data

Riahi-Belkaoui, Ahmed.
    Performance results in value added reporting / Ahmed Riahi-
Belkaoui.
        p.   cm.
    Includes bibliographical references and index.
    ISBN 1–56720–024–9 (alk. paper)
    1. Financial statements.   2. Value added—Accounting.   3. Income
accounting.   4. Corporations—Accounting.   5. International business
enterprises—Accounting.   I. Title.
HF5681.B2R426   1996
657—dc20   95–46276

British Library Cataloguing in Publication Data is available.

Library of Congress Catalog Card Number: 95–46276
ISBN: 1–56720–024–9

First published in 1996

Quorum Books, 88 Post Road West, Westport, CT 06881
An imprint of Greenwood Publishing Group, Inc.

Printed in the United States of America

The paper used in this book complies with the
Permanent Paper Standard issued by the National
Information Standards Organization (Z39.48–1984).

10 9 8 7 6 5 4 3 2 1

To Janice, Elda, Habiba, Ada, and Hedi

Contents

Exhibits

Preface

Value added reporting calls for the measurement and disclosure of net or gross value added, a measure of the increase in wealth generated by the productive use of a firm's resources before its eventual allocation among the production team of the shareholders, bondholders, labor, and the government. Although its use by the foreign multinational firms is on the increase, this innovative form of reporting is encountering some resistance in the U.S. contest. In 1991, an American Accounting Association special committee looking into the topic of measurement in general suggested the expansion of accounting disclosure to include a value added report. One factor arguing for this form of innovative reporting is its general usefulness to investors, users of information, and policy makers. The purpose of this book is to show the usefulness of value added data in various economic and financial contracts. Various empirical studies presented show in fact that (a) value added can be measured under any of the known price changes models; (b) a value added–based model has a better association with stock returns than an accounting profit-based model, and the valuation model relating accounting return to market return is more complete when relating the total return of the market to the total wealth generated, as measured by the net value added; (c) market return is better explained by value added than either earnings or cash flows; (d) value added–based productivity is useful in understanding the role of accounting variables in the prediction of firm valuation; (e) the adoption of performance plans leads to different profit ability changes in firms that have different ownership structures, owner-controlled versus manager controlled; (f) value added accounting information can supply considerable explanatory power of market risk beyond that provided by earnings or cash flow measures, especially at the individual firm level; (g) value added to total assets of acquired firms relative to the average for their industries is positively related to total value created for their stockholders during the takeover; and (h) whether ownership structures are measured by management stockholding, stock concentration, or the sum of the two measures, value added–based performance declines up to a point before increasing proportionally to the increases in ownership structure measures. All these results point to the need for an accounting policy requiring U.S. firms to disclose a value added report or at least the underlying data needed to calculate value added variables.

The book should be of value to all those interested in disclosure issues, including professional accountants, business executives, teachers and researchers, and students.

Many people have helped in the development of this book. I received considerable assistance from the University of Illinois at Chicago research assistants, especially Claire Howard and Birute Pabedinskas. I also thank Eric Valentine and the entire production team at Quorum Books for their continuous and intelligent support. Finally, to Janice and Hedi, thanks for making everything possible and enjoyable.

Chapter 1

Value Added Reporting under Price Change Models

INTRODUCTION

Various sources have supported the coverage of international accounting issues in the curriculum of college and university accounting programs.[1,2] One fundamental issue is the measurement of changes in wealth. Given some of the known limitations of accounting profit as a measure of changes in wealth, international accounting proposals call generally for a consideration of both value added reporting and accounting for inflation as potential useful alternatives.[3]

Value added reporting advocates the measurement and disclosure of value added, the increase in wealth generated by the productive use of the firm's resources before its allocation among shareholders, bondholders, workers, and the government. Its use by European firms is on the increase.[4] Its potential use in the United States has generated favorable positions.[5, 6] Justification of its potential use in the United States is supported by empirical research. Although the disclosure of a value added statement is not mandatory, its derivation is possible if adequate information on the distribution of value added is available from the income statement or other sources. Gray and Maunders[7] recommend, however, that inflation (price level change) adjustments are necessary if net value added is to be meaningful. Coverage of value added reporting in international accounting courses needs to be integrated with the asset valuation alternatives required by the different price change models. Accordingly, this chapter illustrates the derivation of a value added statement under different price change models.

VALUE ADDED REPORTING AND ACCOUNTING FOR INFLATION

Value Added Reporting

As a supplement to the income statement, the value added statement is viewed as a report on the income earned by a larger group of "stakeholders"—all providers of capital plus employees and government.[8] It can be obtained by the following rearrangement of the income statement:

$$S - B = W + I + DP + DDT + T + R \tag{1}$$

or

$$S - B - DP = W + I + DD + T + R \tag{2}$$

where

R = retained earnings,

S = sales revenue,

B = bought-in material and services,

DP = depreciation,

W = wages,

I = interest,

DD = dividends, and

T = taxes.

Equation (1) expresses the gross value added, whereas equation (2) expresses the net value added. In both equations, the left side (the subtractive side) shows the value added (gross or net), and the right side (the additive side) shows the disposal of value added among the stakeholders. A number of academic writers support the net value added concept for a variety of reasons.[9, 10, 11]

Price Change Models

Various models have been proposed to deal with the effects of changing prices on a firm. The debate centers on the merits of the conventional historical cost model versus some form of current value. The differences between the price change models arise from the different attributes to be measured and the units of measure to be used. The attributes of assets and liabilities, referring to what is being measured, include mainly (a) historical cost, (b) replacement cost, and (c) net realizable value. In addition, financial accounting measurements may be made in one of two units of measure: units of money or units of general purchasing power. Combining the three attributes and the two units of measure yields the following six price change models:

1. *Historical cost accounting* measures historical cost in units of money.
2. *Replacement cost accounting* measures replacement cost in units of money.
3. *Net realizable value accounting* measures net realizable value in units of money.
4. *General price level historical cost accounting* measures historical cost in units of purchasing power.
5. *General price level replacement cost accounting* measures replacement cost in units of purchasing power.
6. *General price level net realizable value accounting* measures net realizable value in units of purchasing power.[12]

These six price change models are used in the derivations of the value added statement of a fictional example.

Fictional Example

To illustrate the derivation of the value added statement under the different price change models, let us consider the simplified case of the Hellenic Company, which was formed January 1, 19X6, to distribute a new product called "KALLIOPI." Capital is composed of $3,000 equity and $3,000 liabilities carrying a 5 percent interest. On January 1, the Hellenic Company began operations by purchasing 600 units of KALLIOPI at $10 per unit. On May 1, the company sold 500 units at $15 per unit. At the end of the year, the company made the following cash payments:

1. Interest	=	$150
2. Wages	=	30
3. Taxes	=	100
4. Dividends	=	20

Changes in the general and specific price levels for the year 19X6 are as follows:

	January 1	May 1	December 31
Replacement Cost	$10	$12	$13
Net Realizable Value	—	$15	$17
General Price-Level Index	$100	$130	$156

VALUE ADDED STATEMENTS EXPRESSED IN UNITS OF MONEY

Historical Cost

Historical cost accounting, or conventional accounting, is characterized primarily by (1) the use of historical cost as the attribute of the elements of financial statements, (2) the assumption of a stable monetary unit, (3) the matching principle, and (4) the realization principle. The derivation of the income statements and the value added statement under historical cost accounting is shown, respectively, in Exhibits 1.1 and 1.2. The net value added after gains and losses is equal to $2,500, which is the net wealth generated by the firm using the assumption of historical costs expressed in units of money. It includes a plowback to the firm of $2,200. The $2,200 represents the income reinvested after distribution to shareholders, bondholders, employers, and the government. It contains $700 timing errors because (1) it includes in a single figure operating income and holding gains and losses that are recognized in current period and that occurred in previous periods and (2) it omits the operating profit and holding gains and losses that occurred in the current period but are recognizable in future periods. Second it contains measuring unit errors because (1) it does not take into account changes in the general price level that would have resulted in amounts expressed in units of general purchasing power and (2) by relying on historical cost as the attribute of the elements of financial statements rather than either replacement

Exhibit 1.1
Hellenic Company Income Statements Expressed in Units of Money

INCOME STATEMENTS	HISTORICAL COST	REPLACEMENT COST	NET REALIZABLE VALUE
REVENUES	(1) $7,500	$7,500	(2) $9,200
MINUS EXPENSES:			
A. COST OF MATERIALS	(3) $5,000	(4) $6,000	(5) $7,300
B. INTEREST	$150	$150	$150
C. WAGES	$30	$30	$30
OPERATING PROFIT	$2,320	$1,320	$1,720
REALIZED HOLDING GAINS & LOSSES	INCL. ABOVE	(6) $1,000	$1,000
UNREALIZED HOLDING GAINS & LOSSES	NOT APPLICABLE	(7) $300	$300
GENERAL PRICE LEVEL GAINS & LOSSES	NOT APPLICABLE	NOT APPLICABLE	NOT APPLICABLE
NET PROFIT BEFORE TAX	$2,320	$2,620	$3,020
- TAXES	$100	$100	$100
NET PROFIT AFTER TAXES	$2,220	$2,520	$2,920
- DIVIDENDS	$20	$20	$20
RETAINED EARNINGS	$2,200	$2,500	$2,900

(1) 500 × $15 = $7,500.
(2) 7,500 + ($17 × 100) = $9,200.
(3) 500 × $10 = $5,000.
(4) 500 × $12 = $6,000.
(5) 6,000 + ($13 × 100) = $7,300.
(6) 500 ($12 − $10) = $1,000.
(7) 100 ($13 − $10) = $3,000.

cost or net realizable value, it does not take into account changes in the specific price level. In summary, the net value added under historical cost accounting contains timing and measuring unit errors.

Replacement Cost

Replacement cost accounting is characterized by (1) the use of replacement cost as the attribute of financial statements, (2) the assumption

Exhibit 1.2
Hellenic Company Value Added Statements Expressed in Units of Money

VALUE ADDED STATEMENTS	HISTORICAL COST	REPLACEMENT COST	NET REALIZABLE VALUE
A. SOURCE OF NET VALUE ADDED			
REVENUES	$7,500	$7,500	$9,200
- COST OF MATERIAL	$5,000	$6,000	$7,300
NET VALUE ADDED BEFORE GAINS & LOSSES	$2,500	$1,500	$1,900
REALIZED HOLDING GAINS & LOSSES	INCL. ABOVE	$1,000	$1,000
UNREALIZED HOLDING GAINS & LOSSES	NOT APPLICABLE	$300	$300
GENERAL PRICE LEVEL GAINS & LOSSES	NOT APPLICABLE	NOT APPLICABLE	NOT APPLICABLE
NET VALUE ADDED AFTER GAINS & LOSSES	$2,500	$2,800	$3,200
B. DISTRIBUTION OF NET VALUE ADDED			
INTEREST TO BONDHOLDERS	$150	$150	$150
WAGES TO EMPLOYEES	$30	$30	$30
RETAINED EARNINGS TO FIRM	$2,200	$2,500	$2,900
TAXES TO GOVERNMENT	$100	$100	$100
DIVIDENDS TO SHAREHOLDERS	$20	$20	$20
NET VALUE ADDED AFTER GAINS & LOSSES	$2,500	$2,800	$3,200

of a stable monetary unit, (3) the realization principle, (4) the dichoto-mization of realized and unrealized holding gains and losses. The deri-vation of the income statement and the value added statement under replacement cost accounting is shown, respectively, in Exhibits 1.1 and 1.2. The net value added after gains and losses amounts to $2,800, which is the net wealth generated by the firm under the assumption of replace-ment cost expressed in units of money. It includes a plowback to the firm of $2,500. The $2,500 amount represents the income reinvested after distribution to shareholders, bondholders, employers, and the government. It contains $400 timing errors because (1) it omits the operating profit that occurred in the current period but that is realizable in future periods, (2) it includes the operating profit that is recognized in the current period but that occurred in previous periods, (3) it does not take into account changes in the general price level that would have resulted in amounts expressed in units of general purchasing power, and (4) it does take into account changes in the specific price level because it relies on replacement cost as the attribute of the elements of financial statements. In summary, the net value added under replacement cost accounting contains (1) operation profit timing errors and (2) measuring unit errors.

Net Realizable Value

Net realizable value accounting is characterized primarily by (1) the use of net realizable value as the attribute of the elements of financial statements, (2) the assumption of a stable monetary unit, (3) the abandonment of the realization principle, and (4) the dichotomization of operating income and holding gains and losses. The derivation of the income statement and the value added statement under net realizable value accounting is shown, respectively, in Exhibits 1.1 and 1.2. The net value added after gains and losses amounts to $3,200. It includes a plowback to the firm of $2,900. The $2,900 amount represents the income reinvested after distribution to shareholders, bondholders, employers, and the government. It does not contain any timing errors because (1) it reports all operating profit and holding gains and losses in the same period in which they occur and (2) it excludes all operating and holding gains and losses occurring in previous periods. It contains measuring unit errors because (1) it does not take into account changes in the general price level and (2) it does take into account changes in the specific price level because it relies on net realizable value as the attribute of the elements of financial statements. In summary the net value added under net realizable value accounting contains no timing errors but contains measuring unit errors.

VALUE ADDED STATEMENTS IN UNITS OF PURCHASING POWER

Historical Cost

General price level–adjusted historical cost accounting is characterized primarily by (1) the use of historical cost as the attribute of the elements

Exhibit 1.3
Hellenic Company Income Statements Expressed in Units of Purchasing Power

INCOME STATEMENTS	HISTORICAL COST	REPLACEMENT COST	NET REALIZABLE VALUE
REVENUES	(1) $9,000	$9,000	(2) $10,700
MINUS EXPENSES:			
A. COST OF MATERIALS	(3) $7,800	(4) $7,200	(5) $8,500
B. INTEREST	$150	$150	$150
C. WAGES	$30	$30	$30
OPERATING PROFIT	$1,020	$1,620	$2,020
REAL REALIZED HOLDING GAINS & LOSSES	INCL. ABOVE	(6) ($600)	($600)
REAL UNREALIZED HOLDING GAINS & LOSSES	NOT APPLICABLE	(7) ($260)	($260)
GENERAL PRICE LEVEL GAINS & LOSSES	(8) $180	$180	$180
NET PROFIT BEFORE TAX	$1,200	$940	$1,340
- TAXES	$100	$100	$100
NET PROFIT AFTER TAXES	$1,100	$840	$1,240
- DIVIDENDS	$20	$20	$20
RETAINED EARNINGS	$1,080	$820	$1,220

(1) $7,500 × 156/130 = $9,000.
(2) $9,000 + ($17 × 100 units) = $10,700.
(3) $5,000 × 156/100 = $7,800.
(4) $6,000 × 156/130 = $7,200.
(5) $7,200 + ($13 × 100 units) = $8,500.
(6) [(12 × 156/130) − ($10 × 156/100)] × 500 = ($600).
(7) [13 − ($10 × 156/100)] × 100 units = ($260).
(8) See Exhibit 1.5.

of financial statements, (2) the use of units of general purchasing power as the unit of measure, (3) the matching principle, and (4) the realization principle. The derivation of the income statement and the value added statement under general price level–adjusted historical cost accounting is shown, respectively, in Exhibits 1.3–1.5. The net value added after gains and losses amounts to $1,380. It includes a plowback of $1,080. The $1,080 amount represents the income reinvested after distribution to

Exhibit 1.4
Hellenic Company Value Added Statements Expressed in Units of Purchasing Power

VALUE ADDED STATEMENTS	HISTORICAL COST	REPLACEMENT COST	NET REALIZABLE VALUE
A. SOURCE OF NET VALUE ADDED			
REVENUES	$9,000	$9,000	$10,700
- COST OF MATERIALS	$7,800	$7,200	$8,500
NET VALUE ADDED BEFORE GAINS & LOSSES	$1,200	$1,800	$2,200
REALIZED HOLDING GAINS & LOSSES	INCL. ABOVE	($600)	($600)
UNREALIZED HOLDING GAINS & LOSSES	NOT APPLICABLE	($260)	($260)
GENERAL PRICE LEVEL GAINS & LOSSES	$180	$180	$180
NET VALUE ADDED AFTER TAXES	$1,380	$1,120	$1,520
B. DISTRIBUTION OF NET VALUE ADDED			
INTEREST TO BONDHOLDERS	$150	$150	$150
WAGES TO EMPLOYEES	$30	$30	$30
RETAINED EARNINGS TO FIRM	$1,080	$820	$1,220
TAXES TO GOVERNMENT	$100	$100	$100
DIVIDENDS TO SHAREHOLDERS	$20	$20	$20
NET VALUE ADDED AFTER GAINS & LOSSES	$1,380	$1,120	$1,520

shareholders, bondholders, employers, and the government. It contains the same type of timing errors as under historical cost accounting. It contains no measuring unit errors because it does take into account changes in the general price level. It does not, however, take into account changes in the specific price level because it relies on historical cost as the attribute of the elements of financial statements rather than on replacement cost or net realizable value. In summary, the net value under general price level–adjusted historical cost accounting contains timing errors but does not contain measuring unit errors.

Exhibit 1.5
General Price Level Gain or Loss, December 31, 19X6

	UNADJUSTED	CONVERSION FACTOR	ADJUSTED
NET-MONETARY ASSETS ON JAN 1, 19X6	$3,000	156/100	$4,680
ADD MONETARY RECEIPTS DURING 19X6: SALES	$7,500	156/100	$9,000
NET MONETARY ITEMS	$10,500		$13,680
LESS MONETARY PAYMENTS:			
PURCHASES	$6,000	156/100	$9,360
INTEREST	$150	156/156	$150
WAGES	$30	156/156	$30
TAXES	$100	156/156	$100
DIVIDEND	$20	156/156	$20
TOTAL	$6,300		$9,660
COMPUTED NET MONETARY ASSETS, DEC 31, 19X6			$4,020
ACTUAL NET MONETARY ASSETS, DEC 31, 19X6			$4,200
GENERAL PRICE LEVEL GAIN			$180

Replacement Cost

General price level–adjusted replacement cost accounting is characterized primarily by (1) the use of replacement cost as the attribute of the elements of financial statements, (2) the use of units of general purchasing power as the unit measure, (3) the realization principle, (4) the dichotomization of operating income and real realized holding gains and losses, and (5) the dichotomization of real realized and real unrealized holding gains and losses. The derivation of the income statement and the value added statement under general price level–adjusted replacement cost accounting appears, respectively, in Exhibits 1.3–1.5. The net value added after gains and losses amounts to $1,120. It includes a plowback of $820. The $820 amount represents the income reinvested after distribution to shareholders, bondholders, employees, and the government. It contains the same type of timing errors found under replacement cost accounting. It contains no measuring unit errors because it takes into account changes in the general price level. In addition, it takes into account changes in the specific price level because it adopts replacement cost as the attribute of the elements of financial statements. In summary, the net value added under general price level–adjusted replacement cost contains timing errors but contains no measuring unit errors.

Net Realizable Value

General price level–adjusted net realizable value accounting is characterized primarily by (1) the use of net realizable value as the attribute of the elements of financial statements, (2) the use of units of general purchasing power as the unit of measure, (3) the abandonment of the realization principle, (4) the dichotomization or operation income and real holding gains and losses, and (5) the dichotomization of the real realized and unrealized gains and losses. The derivation of the income statement and the value added statement under general price level–adjusted net realizable value accounting appears, respectively, in Exhibits 1.3–1.5. The net value added after gains and losses amounts to $1,520. It includes a plowback of $1,220. The $1,220 amount represents the income reinvested after distribution to shareholders, bondholders, employees, and the government. It contains no timing errors and no measuring unit errors.

CONCLUSIONS

The application of the different price change models resulted in different values for the net value added. As shown in Exhibit 1.6, there are six different values for net value added. These values are evaluated in terms of whether or not both timing error and measuring unit error are eliminated. The net value added of $1,520, under general price level–adjusted net realizable value accounting, contains nothing from the two errors. It is the ideal measure of net value added under a situation of organized and proper liquidation. Another useful measure is the net value added of $1,120 obtained under general price level–adjusted replacement cost accounting. It indicates the wealth created under operating rather than liquidating conditions after accounting for both changes in the general and specific price level.

Whatever the choice made of these six net value added measures, it is important for the student and the user to understand the various assumptions made in the choice of the attribute and the choice of the measuring unit.

Exhibit 1.6
Error Type Analysis

ACCOUNTING MODEL	NET INCOME	NET VALUE ADDED	TIMING ERROR OPERATING PROFIT	ERROR HOLDING GAINS	MEASURING UNIT ERRORS
1. HISTORICAL COST ACCOUNTING	$2,200	$2,500	YES	YES	YES
2. REPLACEMENT COST ACCOUNTING	$2,500	$2,800	YES	ELIMI- NATED	YES
3. NET REALIZABLE VALUE ACCOUNTING	$2,900	$3,200	ELIMI- NATED	ELIMI- NATED	ELIMI- NATED
4. GENERAL PRICE LEVEL ADJUSTED, HISTORICAL COST ACCOUNTING	$1,080	$1,380	YES	YES	ELIMI- NATED
5. GENERAL PRICE LEVEL ADJUSTED, REPLACEMENT COST ACCOUNTING	$820	$1,120	YES	ELIMI- NATED	ELIMI- NATED
6. GENERAL PRICE LEVEL ADJUSTED, NET REALIZABLE VALUE ACCOUNTING	$1,220	$1,520	ELIMI- NATED	ELIMI- NATED	ELIMI- NATED

NOTES

1. Mintz, S. M., "Internationalization of the Accounting Curriculum," *The International Journal of Accounting Education and Research* (Fall 1980): 137–151.

2. Sherman, W. R., "Internationalization of Accounting Curriculum: Implementation of the Worldwide Dimension Requirement," *Journal of Accounting Education* (Fall 1987): 259–276.

3. Riahi-Belkaoui, A., *Value Added Reporting: Lessons for the United States* (Westport, CT: Greenwood Press, 1992).

4. Meek, G., and S. J. Gray, "The Value Added Statement: An Innovation for U.S. Companies?" *Accounting Horizons* (June 1988): 73–81.

5. Morley, M. F., "The Value Added Statement in Britain," *The Accounting Review* (July 1979): 618–689.

6. American Accounting Association, "Committee on Accounting and Auditing Measurement, 1989–1990," *Accounting Horizons* (September 1991): 81–105.

7. Gray, S. and K. Maunders, *Value Added Reporting: Uses and Measurement* (London: The Association of Certified Accountants, 1980).

8. Meek and Gray, 75.

9. Morley, M. F., "The Value Added Statement: A British Innovation," *The Chartered Accountant Magazine* (May 1978): 31–34.

10. Morley, M. F., "Value Added Reporting," in *Developments in Financial Reporting,* ed. Thomas A. Lee (London: Philip Allan, 1981), 251–269.

11. Rutherford, B. A., "Value Added as a Focus of Attention for Financial Reporting: Some Conceptual Problems," *Accounting and Business Research* (Summer 1977): 215–220.

12. Other price models have been used in the academic literature. They have not reached the degree of acceptance of the six models examined in this study. See, for example, Chasteen, Lanny, "A Taxonomy of Price Change Models," *The Accounting Review* (July 1984): 515–523; Riahi-Belkaoui, Ahmed, *Accounting Theory,* 3rd ed. (London: Academic Press, 1993).

REFERENCES

American Accounting Association. "Committee in Accounting and Auditing Measurement, 1989–1990." *Accounting Horizons* (September 1991): 81–105.

Bannister, James W., and Ahmed Riahi-Belkaoui. "Value Added and Corporate Control in the U.S." *Journal of International Financial Management and Accounting* (Autumn 1991): 241–257.

Bao, Ben-Hsien and Da-Hsien. "An Empirical Investigation of the Association Between Productivity and Firm Value." *Journal of Business Finance and Accounting* (Winter 1989): 699–717.

Chasteen, Lanny. "A Taxonomy of Price Change Models." *The Accounting Review* (July 1984): 515–523.

Gray, Sidney J., and K. T. Maunders. *Value Added Reporting: Uses and Measurement.* London: The Association of Certified Accountants, 1980.

Karpik, Philip, and Ahmed Belkaoui. "The Relative Relationship Between Systematic Risk and Value Added Variables." *Journal of International Financial Management and Accounting* (Autumn 1989): 259–276.

Meek, Gary, and Sidney J. Gray. "The Impact of Stock Market and Corporate Globalization on Disclosure Trends in International Financial Reporting." In *Changing International Financial Markets and Their Impact on Accounting,* 43–66. Champaign, IL: Center for International Education and Research in Accounting, 1992.

———. "The Value Added Statement: An Innovation for U.S. Companies?" *Accounting Horizons* (June 1988): 73–81.

Mintz, S. M. "Internationalization of the Accounting Curriculum." *The International Journal of Accounting Education and Research* (Fall 1980): 137–151.

Morley, M. F. "The Value Added Statement: A British Innovation." *The Chartered Accountant Magazine* (May 1978): 31–34.

————. "The Value Added Statement in Britain." *The Accounting Review* (July 1979): 618–689.

————. "Value Added Reporting." In *Developments in Financial Reporting,* edited by Thomas A. Lee, 251–269. London: Philip Allan, 1981.

Riahi-Belkaoui, Ahmed. *Accounting Theory.* 3rd ed. London: Academic Press, 1993.

————. "Earnings-Returns Relation Versus Net Value Added-Returns Relations: The Case for Nonlinear Specification." *Advances in Quantitative Analysis in Finance and Accounting* (Forthcoming).

————. "The Information Content of Value Added, Earnings and Cash Flows: U.S. Evidence." *The International Journal of Accounting* 28, no. 2 (1993): 140–146.

————. *Value Added Reporting: Lessons for the United States.* Westport, CT: Greenwood Press, 1992.

Rutherford, B. A. "Value Added as a Focus of Attention for Financial Reporting: Some Conceptual Problems." *Accounting and Business Research* (Summer 1977): 215–220.

Sherman, W. R. "Internationalization of the Accounting Curriculum: Implementation of the Worldwide Dimension Requirement." *Journal of Accounting Education* (Fall 1987): 259–276.

Chapter 2

Information Content of Value Added Data

INTRODUCTION

Value added reporting is presented in the international accounting literature as a viable alternative and/or a supplement to the conventional income and cash flow statements. It is an accounting measure of the wealth attributable to all of the firm's stakeholders (equity holders, creditors, employees, and governmental taxing units). Its eventual introduction in the U.S. reporting system has been recommended by the American Accounting Association (AAA) Committee on Accounting and Auditing Measurement.[1] An important argument for its incorporation in the U.S. reporting system rests on its information content in terms of its relation to market return. Accordingly, this chapter investigates two research questions. First, it investigates whether the level of net value added or the changes in net value added divided by the price at the beginning of the stock return period are relevant for evaluating net value added/returns associations. A book value model and a wealth valuation model are used to motivate the net value added/returns associations. Second, it assesses the incremental information content of the disclosure of nonearnings components of value added released concurrently with earnings.

Portions of Chapter 2 are adapted from: Riahi-Belkaoui, Ahmed, and Ronald D. Picur, "Explaining Market Returns: Earnings Versus Value Added Data," *Managerial Finance*, 20, no. 9 (1994): 44–55. Reprinted with permission.

THE RELATIONS BETWEEN NET VALUE ADDED AND RETURNS

Returns and Net Value Added Associations Based on a Book Value Model

A book valuation model expresses the relationship between price and book value, both measures of the "stock" value of the shareholders' equity, as follows:

$$P_{jt} = BV_{jt} + u_{jt} \tag{1}$$

where P_{jt} is the price per share of firm j at time t, BV_{jt} is the book value per share of firm j at time t, and u_{jt} is the difference between P_{jt} and BV_{jt}.

The generation of wealth and the corresponding returns generated, both value variables, are expressed by the following equation:

$$\Delta P_{jt} = \Delta BV_{jt} + u'_{jt} \tag{2}$$

where as defined in equations (1) and (2),

$$\Delta BV_{jt} = NVA_{jt} - d_{jt} \tag{3}$$

where d_{jt} is dividends paid per share over time period $t - 1$ to t, and NVA is net value added.

Deflating equation (3) by P_{jt-1}, beginning-of-period price, yields

$$R_{jt} = NVA_{jt}/P_{t-1} + u''_{jt} \tag{4}$$

where

$$R_{jt} = (AP_{jt} + d_{jt})/P_{t-1}$$

Finally, assuming that prices reflect information that is included in past times series of levels of net value added yields

$$R_{jt} = \alpha_{t0} + \alpha_{t1} NVA_{jt}/P_{t-1} + \alpha_{t2} NVA_{jt-1} + \alpha_{t3} NVA_{jt-2}/P_{t-1}$$
$$+ \alpha_{t4} NVA_{jt-3}/P_{t-1} + \alpha_{t5} NVA_{jt-4}/P_{t-1} + E_{jt} \tag{5}$$

Returns and Net Value Added Associations Based on a Wealth Model

An alternative model expresses price as a multiple of wealth or net value added; that is,

$$P_{jt} = \rho NVA_{jt} + v_{jt} \tag{6}$$

If a dividend is paid on security j at time t, equation (3) becomes

$$P_{jt} + d_{jt} = \rho NVA_{jt} + v^1_{jt} \tag{7}$$

Over time, the flow relation yields

$$P_{jt} + d_{jt} = \rho ANVA_{jt} + v^2_{jt} \tag{8}$$

Deflating equation (8) by P_{jt-1}, beginning-of-period price, yields

$$R_{jt} = \rho(ANVA_{jt}/P_{jt-1}) + v^3_{jt} \tag{9}$$

Finally assuming that prices reflect information on past times series of changing in net value added yields

$$R_{jt} = \alpha_{t0} + \alpha_{t1} (NVA_{jt} - NVA_{t-1}) P_{jt-1}$$
$$+ \alpha_{t2} (NVA_{jt-1} - NVA_{jt-2})/P_{jt-1}$$
$$+ \alpha_{t3} (NVA_{jt-2} - NVA_{jt-3})/P_{jt-1}$$
$$+ \alpha_{t4} (NVA_{jt-3} - NVA_{jt-4})/P_{jt-1}$$
$$+ \alpha_{t5} (NVA_{jt-4} - NVA_{jt-5}) P_{jt-1} + E_{jt} \tag{10}$$

Data and Sample Selection

The net value added data were computed from Compustat data items as follows: net value added (NVA) = the sum of labor expenses, corporate taxes, dividends, interest expenses, and minority shareholders in subsidiaries plus retained earnings.[2]

The security returns, R_{jt}, were computed from the Center for Security Price (CRSP) returns file.

The sample is selected from the period 1982–1991 using the criteria: (i) data needed for the computation of NVA are available on the 1991 Compustat Primary, Secondary, Tertiary, and Full Coverage Annual Industrial File; (ii) security price and the factor to adjust for stock splits and stock dividends are available on the CRSP file.

The selection procedures resulted in a sample of 5,369 firm-year observations. Earnings and price variables are adjusted for stock splits and stock dividends.

Empirical Analyses

The regression models, equations (5) and (10) are estimated for the pooled cross-section and time-series sample as well as for each year of available data. The results from regressions (5) and (10) are reprinted, respectively, in Exhibits 2.1 and 2.2. For the regressions using the pooled sample of all 5,369 firm-year observations, the coefficients are significantly different from zero at the 0.01 level in most cases. The R^2 from the pooled regression based on the levels model in equation (5) is 21.16 percent compared to the R^2 of 20.12 percent from the equivalent regression for the changes model in equations (10).[3] For the year-to-year regressions, the models in equations (5) and (10) were significant in all but one of the 10 cases. Similarly, the R^2 from the levels is higher than the R^2 from the changes model in all cases but one.[4]

The results of this study indicate that (a) both the levels of net value added and the changes in net value added deflated by beginning-of-period price play a role in security valuation, (b) both past periods' levels of net value added and changes in net value added possess significant explanatory power for the current period's stock returns, and (c) the net value added based model has a better association with stock returns (based on R^2) than net value added based changes model.

EVIDENCE ON THE INFORMATIONAL CONTENT OF THE DISCLOSURE OF NET VALUE ADDED COMPONENTS MADE CONCURRENTLY WITH EARNINGS

The purpose of this section is to extend the relevance findings by assessing the incremental information content of the disclosure of non-

Exhibit 2.1
Simple Regression of Annual Security Returns on Current and Past Deflated NVA Levels

NVA LEVELS: $R_{jt} = \alpha_{t0} + \alpha_{t1} NVA_{jt}/P_{t-1} + \alpha_{t2} NVA_{jt-1}/P_{t-1} + \alpha_{t3} NVA_{jt-2}/P_{t-1} + \alpha_{t4} NVA_{jt-3}/p_{t-1} + \alpha_{t5} NVA_{jt-4}/P_{t-1} + \xi_{jt}$

PERIOD	α_{t0}	α_{t1}	α_{t2}	α_{t3}	α_{t4}	α_{t5}	R2	F	N
1982–91	0.1589 (7.962)*	0.0081 (26.603)*	0.0015 (3.283)*	−0.0012 (−2.758)*	−0.0013 (−2.575)*	0.0019 (3.92)*	21.16%	287.93*	5369
1982	0.2937 (16.33)*	0.0016 (2.417)*	0.0021 (2.833)*	−0.004 (−6.953)*	0.00018 (0.165)	−0.0031 (−4.399)*	22.25%	25.071*	443
1983	0.2039 (5.612)*	−0.001 (−1.124)	−0.0003 (−0.685)	−0.0047 (−4.776)*	−0.0013 (−1.31)	0.0035 (2.874)*	9.91%	10.007*	460
1984	0.0119 (0.915)	0.0018 (1.869)***	0.0001 (0.426)	0.0004 (1.165)	−0.0008 (−0.955)	0.0004 (0.587)	2.56%	2.533**	490
1985	0.4611 (2.77)*	0.0008 (0.111)	−0.0017 (−0.278)	0 (−0.003)	−0.0004 (−0.101)	−0.0014 (−0.178)	0.40%	0.037	510
1986	0.0537 (2.416)*	0.0037 (3.37)*	0.0012 (1.076)	0.0011 (0.973)	−0.0004 (−0.619)	0.003 (3.8)*	6.15%	6.757*	521
1987	−0.1163 (−7.304)*	0.004 (5.936)*	−0.0008 (−1.71)*	−0.0024 (−3.555)*	−0.001 (−1.286)	0.0004 (0.832)	8.69%	10.39*	551
1988	0.1455 (5.98)*	0.0078 (18.84)*	−0.007 (−10.14)*	−0.0033 (−5.704)*	0.0023 (2.425)*	−0.0004 (−0.615)	10.50%	68.97*	574
1989	0.1799 (1.263)*	0.0004 (0.918)	0.0001 (0.501)	0 (−0.168)	0.0004 (1.228)	0.0013 (2.613)*	1.97%	2.373**	594
1990	−0.1803 (−15.95)*	0.0008 (3.646)*	0 (−0.2)	−0.0005 (−1.416)	−0.0003 (−1.536)	0.0001 (0.367)	3.54%	4.365*	600
1991	0.556 (7.002)*	0.0001 (0.895)	0.0016 (1.127)	−0.0016 (1.448)	0.0013 (0.815)	0.0004 (0.386)	0.70%	0.864	617
MEAN (2)		0.002 (3.6878)*	−0.00047 (−0.705)	−0.0015 (−1.8989)*	−0.0000 (−0.1174)	0.00042 (0.6267)			

t statistics are provided in parentheses.
*Significant at $\alpha = 0.01$.

Notes:
(1) The test statistics are *t* statistics because the White's test for heteroskedasticity in the residuals revealed no significant heteroskedasticity. When there is (is not) significant heteroskedasticity, the test statistics reported for the intercepts and the slopes are *z* statistics (*t* statistics) appropriate for such cases.
(2) This is the mean of the yearly coefficients, estimated to test for the effect of cross-sectional correlation in the error terms.

Source: Riahi-Belkaoui, Ahmed, and Ronald D. Picur, "Net Value Added as An Explanatory Variable for Returns," *Managerial Finance* 20, no. 9 (1994): 63. Reprinted with permission.

Exhibit 2.2
Simple Regression of Annual Security Returns on Current and Past Deflated NVA Changes

NVA CHANGES: $Rjt = \alpha t0 + \alpha t1(NVAjt - NVAjt{-}1)/Pt{-}1 + \alpha t2(NVAjt{-}1 - NVAjt{-}2)/Pt{-}1 + \alpha t3(NVAjt{-}2 - NVAjt{-}3)/Pt{-}1 + \alpha t4(NVAjt{-}3 - NVAjt{-}4)/pt{-}1 + \alpha t5(NVAjt{-}4 - NVAjt{-}5)/Pt{-}1$

PERIOD	$\alpha t0$	$\alpha t1$	$\alpha t2$	$\alpha t3$	$\alpha t4$	$\alpha t5$	R2	F	N
1982–91	0.1009	0.0078	−0.0057	−0.0026	−0.004	0.0034	20.12%	252.37*	5369
	(4.784)*	(25.878)*	(−16.076)*	(−4.389)*	(−0.618)	(4.927)*			
1982	0.2701	0.0015	−0.0007	−0.0003	−0.0049	0.0018	20.02%	25.616*	443
	(14.791)*	(2.369)*	(−0.836)	(−0.242)	(−2.123)**	(0.02)			
1983	0.1679	−0.0005	0.0005	−0.0049	0.0089	−0.0079	8.34%	13.708*	460
	(7.762)*	(−0.563)	(0.73)	(−4.993)*	(4.878)*	(−12.777)*			
1984	0.0113	0.0018	−0.0017	0.0002	−0.0012	0.0012	2.54%	2.108**	490
	(0.795)	(1.834)***	(−1.2907)	(0.585)	(−1.428)	(1.02)			
1985	0.4851	0.0016	−0.0034	0.0014	−0.0006	−0.0002	0.30%	0.052	510
	(2.699)*	(0.21)	(−0.439)	(0.204)	(−0.141)	(0.0237)			
1986	0.038	0.0036	−0.0022	−0.0003	−0.0013	0.0036	6.10%	6.102*	521
	(1.576)	(3.299)*	(−1.95)**	(−0.204)	(−0.814)	(3.925)*			
1987	−0.1435	0.004	−0.0045	−0.0017	0.0013	0.002	8.19%	11.445*	551
	(−8.362)*	(6.122)*	(−5.944)*	(−2.036)**	(1.4)	(1.947)**			
1988	0.1454	0.0078	−0.0149	0.0037	0.0057	−0.0028	10.50%	53.86*	574
	(5.577)*	(18.345)*	(−34.231)*	(7.171)*	(4.648)*	(−2.509)*			
1989	0.186	0.0007	−0.0006	−0.0003	0.0005	0.0008	1.10%	2.098**	594
	(10.617)*	(1.209)	(−1.071)	(−0.413)	(1.293)	(1.26)			
1990	−0.1919	0.0009	−0.0013	−0.0004	0.0004	0.0005	3.50%	4.658*	600
	(−15.755)*	(3.812)*	(−2.623)*	(−0.963)	(1.02)	(1.794)			
1991	0.5164	0.001	0.0006	−0.0033	0.003	−0.0009	9.69%	0.724	617
	(6.029)*	(0.763)	(0.673)	(−1.207)***	(1.547)	(−0.467)			
MEAN (2)		0.00224	−0.00282	−0.00059	0.0012	−0.00019			
		(3.74)*	(−4.69817)*(−0.2098)		(1.028)**	(−0.57633)			

t statistics are provided in parentheses.

*Significant at $\alpha = 0.01$.

Notes:
(1) The test statistics are *t* statistics because the White's test for heteroskedasticity in the residuals revealed no significant heteroskedasticity. When there is (is not) significant heteroskedasticity, the test statistics reported for the intercepts and the slopes are *z* statistics (*t* statistics) appropriate for such cases.
(2) This is the mean of the yearly coefficients, estimated to test for the effect of cross-sectional correlation in the error terms.

Source: Riahi-Belkaoui, Ahmed, and Ronald D. Picur, "Net Value Added as An Explanatory Variable for Returns," *Managerial Finance* 20, no. 9 (1994): 64. Reprinted with permission.

earnings components of value added released concurrently with annual earnings. We measure informational content in the form of a statistically significant association between disclosure of earnings and nonearnings components of net value added and annual stock returns.

Estimation Model

The net value added, as a measure of wealth, is equal to earnings plus the nonearnings components. Most studies examining the market relevance of accounting data have focused on the informational content of earnings without regard to the other concurrent disclosures that allow the computation of the total wealth generated by the firm. Assuming that the market is uniquely composed of equity holders, the market return will be, as expected, positively related to earnings and negatively related to nonearnings components of net value added. The rationale for the negative sign is the fact that these nonearnings components reduce the amount of wealth to be allocated to equity holders. Accordingly, the return model can be stated as follows:

$$(AP_{jt} + D_{jt})/P_{jt-1} = a_0 + a_1 E_{jt}/N_{jt} - a_2 NE_{jt}/N_{jt} + e_{jt} \tag{11}$$

or

$$(AP_{jt} + D_{jt})/P_{jt-1} = a_0 + a_1 ECW_{jt} - a_2 NECW_{jt} + e_{jt} \tag{12}$$

where P = market price of the security, D = dividend, N = number of shares, ECW = earnings component of wealth, and NECW = nonearnings component of wealth.

The model depicted in equation (12) implies a linear relationship between the annual return of a security on one hand and the earnings and the nonearnings components of wealth on the other. The relationship is expected to be positive with the earnings component and negative with the nonearnings components.

Data and Sample Selection

The accounting return variables used were based on net value added and the earnings and nonearnings components of net value added. More

explicitly, these measures are defined from Compustat data items as follows:

1. Net value added (NVA) = the sum of labor expenses, corporate taxes, dividends, interest expense, minority shareholders in subsidiaries, and retained
   earnings.
2. Earnings (E) = income available to common equity.
3. Nonearnings components of value added (NE) = NVA − E.

The firms examined in this study represent all the New York Stock
Exchange (NYSE) and American Exchange (AMEX) firms that have
available NVA, E, P, N, and D data over the period 1973–1991 on
Compustat. The selection procedure resulted in a sample of observations
ranging between 156 and 220 firms per year.[5]

General Results

The regression model, equation (12), is estimated for each of the
years 1973–1991. The results are presented in Exhibit 2.3. The F statistic shows that the regression is significant each year, at least equal to
0.05. In addition, both the earnings and nonearnings components are
significant for each of the years examined and have the expected sign:
positive for earnings and negative for nonearnings. In addition, the
across-year significance test indicates that both the earnings and the
nonearnings components of wealth, as measured by NVA, are significant at $\alpha = 0.01$.

Impact of Inflation and Growth

Similarly to other studies on the value relevance of accounting data,[6,7]
this section extends the analyses to evaluate the impact of changes in
the macroeconomic variables of inflation and gross national product
(GNP) growth. The inflation and GNP growth levels were measured,
respectively, by (a) the annual change in the Consumers' Price Index,
and (b) the annual change in real GNP. The sample was divided into
three categories of inflation rate and GNP growth rate. The classification
is shown in Exhibit 2.4. Exhibit 2.5 shows the results of regression (12)
for each of the three levels of inflation and GNP growth. The results
show that the significance and the signs of earnings and nonearnings
components are not affected by the levels of inflation and GNP growth.

Exhibit 2.3
Value Relevance of NVA Components

Year	Interest	ECW	NECW	F	R^2	N
1973	-0.11842*	0.00541*	-0.00169**	3.428**	4.34%	180
1974	-0.18352*	0.10896*	-0.00058	7.499*	7.69%	182
1975	0.53347*	0.10307*	-0.00379*	3.833**	4.86%	195
1976	0.33786*	0.02186*	-0.00049	3.440**	3.22%	209
1977	0.11633*	0.12274*	-0.00573*	16.164*	13.34%	212
1978	0.19418*	0.06689*	-0.00350*	4.218*	3.74%	219
1979	0.26850*	0.06641*	-0.00280*	4.079*	3.61%	220
1980	0.27138*	0.24727**	-0.00079	3.289**	3.07%	210
1981	0.05949*	0.00808**	-0.00041*	3.429**	3.42%	201
1982	0.29458*	0.12004**	-0.00116*	2.719**	3.16%	194
1983	0.26669*	0.11078*	-0.00528*	6.158*	6.27%	186
1984	0.01461**	0.19006*	-0.00091**	8.544*	8.63%	183
1985	0.39838*	0.04152**	-0.00399*	6.715*	6.91%	183
1986	0.28429*	0.05207**	-0.00343**	3.407**	3.64%	171
1987	0.17877*	0.17435**	-0.00333**	3.437**	3.80%	176
1988	0.17800*	0.05640*	-0.00051*	4.516*	3.60%	174
1989	0.26623*	0.04465**	-0.00236**	9.918**	3.34%	171
1990	-0.01851*	0.02691**	-0.00159**	3.940**	4.43%	172
1991	0.29137*	0.06666*	-0.00116*	3.773**	4.63%	156
Across Year Means	0.18970*	0.08596*	-0.00288*			
(Value)	23.939*	4.604*	-3.662*			

*Significant at $\alpha = 0.01$.
**Significant at $\alpha = 0.05$.

Exhibit 2.4
Classification of Firms into Categories of Inflation and Growth Levels

Categories	Low	Medium	High
Inflation	1983 (7.2)[1], 1985 (3.6) 1986 (1.9), 1987 (3.6) 1988 (4.1), 1991 (4.2)	1973 (6.7), 1976 (5.8) 1977 (6.5), 1982 (6.2) 1984 (4.3), 1989 (4.8) 1990 (5.4)	1974 (11.0), 1975 (9.1) 1978 (7.0), 1979 (11.3) 1980 (13.5), 1981 (10.3)
GNP Growth	1974 (-0.5)[2], 1975 (-1.1) 1980 (-0.6), 1982 (-2.3) 1990 (1.3), 1991 (-0.9)	1979 (2.8), 1981 (1.6) 1983 (3.8), 1985 (8.9) 1986 (2.8), 1987 (3.0) 1989 (2.7)	1973 (5.4), 1976 (5.1) 1977 (4.6), 1978 (4.8) 1984 (6.0), 1988 (4.0)

[1]The number within parentheses is the change in consumer price index.
[2]The number within parentheses is the change in GNP.

Concluding Remarks

This section presents evidence on the informational content of the disclosure of net value added components made concurrently with earnings. As expected, the earnings component of net value added is viewed favorably by the market, whereas nonearnings components of earnings are negatively related to annual market return. The market as a theater for equity holders views the return to equity holders as positive, whereas the returns to other stakeholders are viewed as a decrease in the net wealth allocated to equity holders, which explains the negative relationship. In any case, the valuation model relating accounting return to market return is more complete when relating the total return of the market to the total wealth generated, as measured by the net value added.

CONCLUSIONS

Taken as a whole, the results of this chapter add to the growing empirical evidence on the market relevance of value added. Thus an important accounting policy issue is the desirability of disclosing the underlying data needed to compute value added variables. The current disclosure system does not mandate the disclosure of some of the information needed to compute the value added. At present, less than 15 percent of the firms listed on Compustat consistently disclose labor ex-

Exhibit 2.5
Impact of Inflation and GNP Growth Levels in the Value Relevance of NVA Components

	Inflation Ratio			GNP Growth		
	High Inflation	Medium Inflation	Low Inflation	High	Medium	Low
Intercept	0.19444*	0.11969*	0.26156*	0.14419*	0.23485*	0.21022*
EPW	0.00785**	0.02598*	0.03500*	0.01811*	0.01691*	0.05106*
NEPW	-0.00039**	- 0.00067**	-0.00042	- 0.00067*	- 0.00088*	- 0.00001**
F	2.958ᴬᴬ	13.009ᴬ	4.407*	6.197*	7.888*	6.031ᴬ
R^2	3.33%	3.93%	3.83%	3.90%	3.19%	3.07%

*Significant at $\alpha = 0.01$.
**Significant at $\alpha = 0.05$.

penses, a key variable. Supplementary financial statements are a practical way for introducing and gaining experience with new kinds of information. Value added concepts are examples of the type of innovation in need of experimentation. More research on its relevance is also needed.

NOTES

1. American Accounting Association, "Committee on Accounting and Auditing Measurement, 1989–1990," *Accounting Horizons* (September 1991): 81–105.

2. Each variable is defined using Compustat's annual individual data as follows:

$$NVA = (42_t + 6_t + 19_t + 21_t + 15_t + 49_t + 36_t - 36_{t-1})$$

3. Because of possible cross-sectional correlation in the regression error in the equation of each of the models, there is potential for bias in statistical inferences regarding the earnings coefficients (see Bernard, 1987). Accordingly, an alternative procedure is used to test the significance of the earnings coefficients by using the mean and standard error of the coefficients obtained from the separate annual regression (with the assumptions that these annual regressions are independent). These calculations are shown in both Exhibits 2.1 and

2.2. All the coefficients are significant indicating that the significance of earnings coefficients is unlikely to result from potential cross-sectional correlations.

4. To check if the results might be affected by collinearity among the variables, condition indices were computed for each regression reported in both tables. Mild collinearity exists if the maximum condition is over 30. The results in this study indicated a condition index with a higher value of 4. Collinearity, therefore, does not seem to affect our results.

5. The sample for each year was trimmed of outliers by 1 percent of each variable. The influential outliers were identified using an observations influence on (a) predicted values of the dependent variable, (b) residuals, (c) the covariance matrix, and (d) the regression fit. The regressions run on the original data were less significant than those on the truncated sample.

6. Wilson, P., ''The Relative Informational Content of Accruals and Cash Flows: Combined Evidence at the Earnings Announcement and Annual Report Release Date,'' *Journal of Accounting Research* (September 1986): 165–200.

7. Bernard, V. L., and T. Stober, ''The Nature and Amount of Information in Cash Flows and Accruals,'' *The Accounting Review* (October 1989): 624–652.

REFERENCES

American Accounting Association. ''Committee on Accounting and Auditing Measurement, 1989–1990.'' *Accounting Horizons* (September 1991): 81–105.

Bannister, J. W., and Ahmed Riahi-Belkaoui. ''Value Added and Corporate Control.'' *Journal of International Financial Management and Accounting* (Autumn 1991): 241–257.

Bao, Ben-Hsien, and Da-Hsien Bao. ''An Empirical Investigation of the Associations Between Productivity and Firm Value.'' *Journal of Business Finance and Accounting* (Winter 1989): 699–717.

Belsley, D. A., E. Kuh, and R. E. Welsh. *Regression Diagnostics: Identifying Influential Data and Sources of Collinearity.* New York: Wiley, 1980.

Bernard, V. L. ''Cross-Sectional Dependence and Problems in Inference in Market-Based Accounting Research.'' *Journal of Accounting Research* (Spring 1987): 1–48.

Bernard, V. L., and T. Stober. ''The Nature and Amount of Information in Cash Flows and Accruals.'' *The Accounting Review* (October 1989): 624–652.

Choi, D.S.F., and G. G. Mueller. *International Accounting.* Englewood Cliffs, NJ: Prentice-Hall, 1992.

Cox, B. *Value Added: An Appreciation for the Accounts Concerned with Industry.* London: Heinemann, 1978.

Financial Accounting Standards Board. *Statement of Financial Accounting Concepts No. 5: Recognition and Measurement in Financial Statements of Business Enterprises.* Stamford, CT: FASB, 1984.

Gray, S., and K. Maunders. *Value Added Reporting: Uses and Measurement.* London: The Association of Certified Accountants, 1980.

Karpik, P., and Ahmed Belkaoui. "The Relative Relationship Between Systematic Risk and Value Added Variables." *Journal of International Financial Management and Accounting* (Autumn 1985): 225–245.

Lev, Baruch. *Financial Statement Analysis: A New Approach.* Englewood Cliffs, NJ: Prentice-Hall, 1974.

Maunders, K. T. "The Decision Relevance of Value Added Reports." In *Frontiers of International Accounting: An Anthology,* edited by F. D. Choi and G. G. Mueller, 225–245. Ann Arbor, MI: UMI Research Press, 1985.

McLeary, S. "Value Added: A Comparative Study." *Accounting Organizations and Society* 8, no. 1 (1983): 31–56.

Meek, G. K., and S. J. Gray. "The Value Added Statement: An Innovation for U.S. Companies?" *Accounting Horizons* (June 1988): 73–81.

———. "The Impact of Stock Market and Corporate Globalization on Disclosure Trends in International Financial Reporting." In *Changing International Financial Markets and Their Impact on Accounting,* 43–66. Champaign, IL: Center for International Education Research in Accounting, 1992.

Morely, M. F. "The Value Added Statement: A British Innovation." *The Chartered Accountant Magazine* (May 1978): 31–34.

———. "The Value Added Statement in Britain." *The Accounting Review* (July 1979): 618–689.

———. "Value Added Reporting." In *Development in Financial Reporting,* edited by Thomas A. Lee, 251–269. London: Philip Allan, 1981.

Renshall, M., R. Allan, and K. Nicholson. *Added Value in External Financial Reporting.* London: Institute of Chartered Accountants in England and Wales, 1979.

Riahi-Belkaoui, Ahmed. "Earnings-Returns Relation Versus Net Value Added-Returns Relation: The Case for Nonlinear Specification," *Advances in Quantitative Analysis of Finance and Accounting* (Forthcoming).

———. "The Information Content of Value Added, Earnings and Cash Flow: U.S. Evidence." *The International Journal of Accounting* 28, no. 2 (1993): 140–146.

———. *Value Added Reporting.* Westport, CT: Quorum, 1992.

Rutherford, B. A. "Value Added as a Focus of Attention for Financial Reporting: Some Conceptual Problems." *Accounting and Business Research* (Summer 1977): 215–220.

Schaeffer, T., and M. Kennelley. "Alternative Cash Flow Measures and Risk-Adjusted Returns." *Journal of Accounting, Auditing and Finance* (Fall 1986): 278–287.

Sinha, G. *Value Added Income.* Calcutta: Book World, 1983.

Suojanen, W. W. "Accounting Today and the Large Corporation." *Accounting Review* (July 1954): 391–398.

White, H. "A Heteroskedasticity-Consistent Covariance Matrix Estimator and a Direct Test for Heteroskedasticity." *Econometrica* (May 1980): 817–838.

Wilson, P. "The Relative Information Content of Accruals and Cash Flows: Combined Evidence at the Earnings Announcement and Annual Report Release Date." *Journal of Accounting Research* (September 1986): 165–200.

Chapter 3

Explaining Market Return: Value Added versus Earnings and Cash Flow

INTRODUCTION

This chapter examines the relationship between market return on the one hand and value added, earnings, and cash flow on the other hand. The objective of the chapter is to present evidence showing the superiority of value added data in explaining market return.

EXPLAINING MARKET RETURNS: EARNINGS VERSUS VALUE ADDED DATA

In this section we investigate whether the relative change in earnings and/or net value added data are relevant for evaluating earnings/returns associations. Previous studies were limited to the association between the market return and either the level of earnings and/or the changes in the level of earnings, both divided by the beginning of the period price.[1] This section differs in two respects. First, in addition to earnings it examines a known and conventional measure of accounting return, net value added, a measure of wealth created and attributable to all stakeholders and advocated as an important European innovation worthy of

Portions of Chapter 3 are adapted from: Riahi-Belkaoui, Ahmed, and M. Ali Fekrat, "The Magic in Value Added: Merits of Derived Accounting Indicator Numbers," *Managerial* Finance, 20, no. 9 (1994): 3–15. Reprinted with permission.

inclusion in U.S. company annual reports. Second, it uses the relative changes in earnings and/or net value added as measures of accounting return rather than the level of earnings only.

Usefulness of Value Added Data

The concern in this chapter is with the relative ability of value added concepts in explaining market return. The following arguments can be used.

First, the earnings/return research shows a limited usefulness of earnings.[2] In addition, the extent of the earnings/return association does not increase considerably when the return window is expanded to one year. The studies that examined the informational contribution of earnings related data provide however an increase in R^2.[3] Value added data represent earnings related data. Those data are typically not available to investors at the time summary earnings information is released, because earnings announcement generally precede, by several weeks, the public release of annual reports and other statements to regulatory agencies. Examining the information content of value added variables is aimed at determining whether information beyond ''bottom line'' earnings is useful, at the margin, in explaining the behavior of share prices. The basic question in need of investigation is whether the more comprehensive value added variables contain information that is relevant to the pricing of securities.

Second, in most of the economic and finance models establishing relationships between firms' earnings or cash flows and their market values, the role of earnings or other financial variables, is to provide investors with information about securities' future returns. The quality of financial variables is then determined by their contributions to the prediction of security returns. This implies that the higher the predictive contribution of value added variables, the higher their quality. This is in line with Lev's suggestion[4] that an operational measure of quality is the ability of the variable to facilitate the prediction of securities' outcomes or to provide for improved portfolio decisions. This is also in line with the Financial Accounting Standards Board's (FASB's) concept of usefulness and quality.

Returns and Earnings Associated Based on a Relative Valuation Model

The conventional earnings valuation model is as follows:

$$(\Delta P_{jt} + D_{jt})/P_{jt-1} = \rho_l(\Delta A_{jt}/P_{t-1}) + U_{jt} \tag{1}$$

where

P_{jt} = market price of the security j at time t,

D_{jt} = dividend of firm j at time t, and

A_{jt} is the accounting earnings of firm j at time t.

The model depicted in equation (1) implies a linear relation between the change in price and the change in earnings deflated by the beginning-of-period price over the period.

A more logical model rests on expressing a relationship between relative changes on both sides of the equation. It follows that

$$(\Delta P_{ji} + D_{ji})/P_{ji-1} = \rho_2(\Delta A_{ji}/A_{ji-1}) = V_{ji} \tag{2}$$

That is, there is a linear relationship between the relative changes in security prices and the relative changes in earnings.

Returns and Earnings Association Based on a Relative Net Value Added Valuation Model

Both equations (1) and (2) still reflect the conventional thesis that the accounting return most associated with security returns is the earnings variable. Following the arguments used earlier that net value added contains information that is relevant to the pricing of securities, the following model is proposed:

$$(\Delta P_{jt} = D_{jt})/P_{jt-1} = \rho_3(\Delta NVA/NVA_{t-1}) + W_{jt} \tag{3}$$

where

NVA = net value added.

Equation (3) illustrates a linear relation between the change in price and the change in net value added data.

Combination of Models

Stock price may be affected by both (a) earnings that signal returns to shareholders and (b) net value added that signals returns to all stockholders, all providers of capital, plus employees and government. By combining an "earnings only" model (similar to equation [2]) and a "net value added only" model (similar to equation [3]), this study proposes a valuation model in which the relative change in process is a weighted function of the relative change of earnings and net value added. It follows that

$$(\Delta P_{jt} + D_{jt})/P_{jt-1} = k\rho_4(\Delta A_{jt}/A_{jt-1})$$
$$+ (1 - k)\rho_5(NVA_{jt}/NVA_{jt-1}) = W_{jt} \qquad (4)$$

where k is a factor for weighting the contribution of the relative change in earnings versus the relative change in net value added in the explanation of stock returns.

Data and Sample Selection

The accounting return variables used were based either on value added or earnings. They were constructed from Compustat data item as follows:

1. Net value added (NVA) = the sum of labor expenses, corporate taxes, dividends, interest expenses, and minority shareholders in subsidies plus retained earnings.
2. Earnings (E) income available to common equity.

The firms examined in this study represent all NYSE and AMEX firms that have available NVA, A, and P data over the period 1979–1983 in Compustat.[5]

This selection procedure resulted in a sample of 2,398 firm-year observations.

Empirical Analysis

Results Based on the Relative Earnings Valuation Model

The regression model based on the relative earnings valuation model is

$$R_{jt} = \alpha_{t0} + \alpha_{t1}RE_{jt} + \varepsilon_{jt}^1 \qquad (5)$$

where

$$R_{jt} = (\Delta P_{jt} + d_{jt})/P_{jt-1},$$
$$RE_{jt} = \Delta E_{jt}/E_{jt-1}, \text{ and}$$
$$E_{jt} = \text{current earnings.}$$

This regression model was estimated for the pooled cross-section and time-series sample as well as for each year (t) of available data. To control for a potential year effect, the regression model on the total sample included dummy variables for each of the years examined. The results using the pooled sample of all 2,398 firm-year observations, shown in Exhibit 3.1, part 1, indicate both α_{t0} and α_{t1} are significant at the 0.01 level. The results for each year are shown in Exhibit 3.2, where both coefficients are shown to be significant. Those results indicate that, as the model in equation (2) suggests, the relative change in security price is associated with the relative change in earnings.

Results Based on the Relative Net Value Added Model

The regression model based on the related net value added model is

$$R_{jt} = \alpha_{t0} + \alpha_{t1}RNVA_{jt} + \varepsilon_{jt}^2 \tag{6}$$

where

$$RNVA_{jt} = \Delta NVA_{jt}/NVA_{jt-1}$$

The results using the pooled sample of 2,398 firm-year observations, shown in Exhibit 3.1, part 2, as well as in the year-by-year regressions, shown in Exhibit 3.3, indicate that both α_{t0} and α_{t1} are significant at the 0.01 level. The adjusted R^2 from the pooled sample using the relative net value added model is 6.6 percent compared to the R^2 of 3.5 percent from the same results using the relative earnings valuation model. Similar adjusted R^2 results are observed for the year-by-year regressions. These findings show that (a) the model in equation (3) suggests that the relative change in security price is associated with the relative change in earnings and (b) models based on the relative net value model provide more explanatory power than models based on the relative earnings models.

Exhibit 3.1
Regression of Annual Security on Relative Changes of Forms of Accounting Returns

Part	Years	Intercept	RNVA	RCE	x_1 (1983)	x_2 (1982)	x_3 (1981)	x_4 (1980)	F	R^2
1	1979–1983	0.079 (4.53)*	+0.2106 (+9.167)*	--------	0.1202 (5.144)*	0.1798 (7.628)*	-0.0372 (-1.685)***	0.052 (2.222)**	33.94*	0.0662
2	1979–1983	0.126 (7.142)*	--------	0.000002 (2.355)**	0.089 (3.826)*	0.1487 (6.338)*	-0.0511 (-2.162)**	0.0406 (1.715)***	17.74*	0.0352
3	1979–1983	0.079 (4.5)*	+0.21111 (+9.1)*	0.000005 (0.665)	0.1206 (5.15)*	0.1799 (7.6)*	-0.0372 (-1.684)***	0.0524 (2.223)**	28.35*	0.0664

t statistics are provided in parentheses.
*Significant at α = 0.01.
**Significant at α = 0.05.
***Significant at α = 0.10.

Source: Riahi-Belkaoui, Ahmed, and Ronald D. Picur, "Explaining Market Returns: Earnings Versus Value Added Data," Managerial Finance 20, no. 9 (1994): 53. Reprinted with permission.

Exhibit 3.2
Simple Regression of Annual Security Returns on Relative Annual Changes in Level of Earnings

$$R_{jt} = \alpha_{t0} + \alpha_{t1} RCE_t + \epsilon_{jt}$$

Year	α_{t0}	α_{t1}	F	R^2
1988	0.27 (2.23)*	+0.00001 (+0.182)	0.033	0.0001
1983	0.23 (11.4)*	-0.000003 (-0.311)	0.097	0.0002
1982	0.276 (15.16)*	+0.048 (+3.06)*	9.36**	0.00018
1981	0.076 (5.17)*	+0.016 (+2.203)**	4.852**	0.010
1980	0.171 (10.44)*	+0.066 (7.012)*	49.16*	0.094
1979	0.1247 (11.01)*	+0.0138 (+1.556)***	1.840	0.0039

t statistics are provided in parentheses.
   *Significant at $\alpha = 0.01$.
  **Significant at $\alpha = 0.05$.
 ***Significant at $\alpha = 0.10$.

Source: Riahi-Belkaoui, Ahmed, and Ronald D. Picur, "Explaining Market Returns: Earnings Versus Value Added Data," *Managerial Finance* 20, no. 9 (1994): 54. Reprinted with permission.

Results Based on the Combination Model

The regression model based on the combination model is

$$R_{jt} = \alpha_{r0} + \alpha_{r1}RNVA + \alpha_{r2}RE + \epsilon_{jt}^3 \tag{7}$$

The results using the pooled sample, shown in Exhibit 3.1, part 3, as well as the results of the year-by-year regressions, shown in Exhibit 3.4, indicate that all the coefficients are significant. The adjusted R^2 from the pooled sample using the combination model is 6.4 percent compared to the adjusted R^2 of 3.5 percent using the relative earnings valuation model and the adjusted R^2 of 6.62 percent using the relative net value added

Exhibit 3.3
Simple Regression of Annual Security Returns on Relative
Annual Changes in Net Value Added

$$R_{jt} = \alpha_{t0} + \alpha_{t1} \, RCNVA_t + \epsilon_{jt}$$

Year	α_{t0}	α_{t1}	F	R^2
1983	0.203 (10.44)*	+0.163 (+3.19)*	10.232*	0.02
1982	0.26 (14.1)*	+0.14 (+3.16)*	9.985*	0.0281
1981	0.01 (1.53)***	+0.34 (-5.774)*	33.33*	0.0657
1980	0.094 (4.4)*	+0.426 (5.524)*	30.5*	0.096
1979	0.078 (5.734)*	+0.216 (-6.83)*	36.36*	0.0733

t statistics are provided in parentheses.
  *Significant at $\alpha = 0.01$.
 **Significant at $\alpha = 0.05$.
***Significant at $\alpha = 0.10$.

Source: Riahi-Belkaoui, Ahmed, and Ronald D. Picur, "Explaining Market Returns: Earnings Versus Value Added Data," *Managerial Finance* 20, no. 9 (1994): 54. Reprinted with permission.

valuation model. Similar results are observed for the year-by-year regressions.

These findings show that (a) as the model in equation (4) suggests, the relative changes in security price are correlated with both the relative changes in earnings and net value added and (b) the combination model shows a better explanatory power than models based on either the net value added or earnings.

THE INFORMATION CONTENT OF VALUE ADDED, EARNINGS, AND CASH FLOW

The suggestions for additional disclosures in U.S. annual reports of value added data in addition to both earnings and cash flow data raise the fundamental question of the incremental and relative information

Exhibit 3.4
Multiple Regression of Annual Security Returns on Relative Annual Changes in Net Value Added and Related Annual Changes in the Level of Earnings

$R_{jt} = \alpha_{t0} + \alpha_{t1}\ RCNVA_t + \alpha_{t2}\ RCE_t + \epsilon_{jt}$				
Year	α_{t0}	α_{t1}	α_{t2}	F	R^2
1983	0.20 (10.4)*	+0.16 (+3.22)*	−0.000005 −(1.611)***	5.2399*	0.0205
1982	0.26 (14.4)*	+0.12 (+2.73)*	+0.04 (+2.57)*	8.36*	0.033
1981	0.021 (1.17)	+0.355 (+5.602)*	+0.012 (+1.67)***	18.126*	0.071
1980	0.115 (5.519)*	+0.324 (+4.24)*	+0.056 (+5.864)*	33.54*	0.1261
1979	0.076 (5.58)*	+0.217 (6.07)*	+0.014 (+1.632)***	19.25*	0.0774

t statistics are provided in parentheses.
  *Significant at α = 0.01.
 **Significant at α = 0.05.
***Significant at α = 0.10.

Source: Riahi-Belkaoui, Ahmed, and Ronald D. Picur, "Explaining Market Returns: Earnings Versus Value Added Data," *Managerial Finance* 20, no. 9 (1994): 54. Reprinted with permission.

content of each of the three measures of accounting return: earnings, cash flows, and value added.

Estimation Model

A generally accepted return valuation model used is as follows:

$$(\Delta P_{jt} + D_{jt})/P_{jt} = a_0 + a_1(\Delta AR_{jt}/AR_{jt}) + e_{jt} \qquad (8)$$

where P = market price of the security, D = dividend, and AR = accounting return (earnings, value added, or cash flow based).

The model depicted in equation (8) implies a linear relation between the relative changes in security prices and the relative change in accounting return (as measured by either the relative change in earnings, value added, or cash flows). The model can be described by either one of the following three equations:

$$\text{RCMR}_{jt} = a_0 + a_1\text{RCE}_{jt} + e_{jt} \tag{8a}$$

$$\text{RCMR}_{jt} = a_0 + a_1\text{RNVA}_{jt} + e_{jt} \tag{8b}$$

$$\text{RCMR}_{jt} = a_0 + a_1\text{RCF}_{jt} + e_{jt} \tag{8c}$$

where RCMR = changes in security price return, RCE = changes in earnings, RNVA = changes in net value added, and RCF = changes in cash flow.

The models depicted in equations (8a), (8b), and (8c) limit the impact of the relative changes in accounting returns on the changes in security prices to the present year and do not include the impact of at least the potential impact of the earlier years. A one-lag model that would include the impact of the preceding year would be as follows:

$$(\Delta P + D_{jt})/P_{jt-1} = a_0 + a_1(\Delta\text{AR}_{jt}/\text{AR}_{jt-1})$$
$$+ a_2(\Delta\text{AR}_{jt-1}/\text{AR}_{jt2}) + e_{jt} \tag{9}$$

Equation (9) depicting the one-lag valuation model will be used as the estimation model in this study for the determination of the relative information content of each of the three accounting return measures considered in this study: earnings, value added, and cash flow. The model can be expressed by one of the following three equations:

$$\text{RCMV}_t = a_0 + a_1\text{RCE}_t + a_2\text{RCE}_{t-1} + e_{jt} \tag{9a}$$

$$\text{RCMV}_t = a_0 + a_1\text{RNVA}_t + a_2\text{RNVA}_{t-1} + e_{jt} \tag{9b}$$

$$\text{RCMV}_t = a_0 + a_1\text{RCF}_t + a_2\text{RCF}_{t-1} + e_{jt} \tag{9c}$$

When examining the information content of two measures of accounting return, AR_1 and AR_2, the following equation will be used:

$$(\Delta P_{jt} + D_{jt})/P_{jt-1} = a_0 + a_1(\Delta AR_{1,jt}/AR_{1,jt-1})$$
$$+ a_2(\Delta AR_{1,jt}/AR_{1,jt-1})$$
$$+ a_3(\Delta AR_{2,jt}/AR_{2,jt-1})$$
$$+ a_4(\Delta AR_{2,jt-1}/AR_{2,jt-2}) + e_{jt} \tag{10}$$

This equation can be described by any one of the following three equations:

$$RCMV_t = a_0 + a_1 RCE_t + a_2 RCE_{t-1} a_3 RVNA_t$$
$$+ a_4 RNVA_{t-1} + e_{jt} \tag{10a}$$

$$RCMV_t = a_0 + a_1 RCE_t + a_2 RCE_{t-1} a_3 RCFE_t$$
$$+ a_4 RCFE_{t-1} + e_{jt} \tag{10b}$$

$$RCMV_t = a_0 + a_1 RNVA_t + a_2 RNVA_{t-1} a_3 RCF_t$$
$$+ a_4 RCFE_{t-1} + e_{jt} \tag{10c}$$

Data and Sample Selection

The accounting return variables used were based on value added, earnings or cash flow measures. More explicitly, these measures are defined from Compustat data items as follows:

1. Net value added (NVA) = the sum of labor expenses, corporate taxes, dividends, interest expense, minority shareholders in subsidiaries, and retained earnings.
2. Earnings (E) = income available to common equity.
3. Cash flow (CF) = cash flows generated from continuing operations, where cash flows are defined as income available to common plus depreciation, deferred taxes, and the changes in the noncash working capital.

The firms examined in this study represent all the NYSE and AMEX firms that have available NVA, E, CF, and P data over the period 1981–1987 in Compustat. The selection procedure resulted in a sample of 4,325 firm-year observations.

Exhibit 3.5
Regression Results on Simple Return Effects

Model 1: Earnings based

	Intercept	RCE$_t$	RCE$_{t-1}$	F	R^2
Coefficient	0.1111	0.0015	0.0022	3.450**	0.0019
t	14.15*	2.334*	1.460***		

Model 2: Net value added based

	Intercept	RNVA$_t$	RNVA$_{t-1}$	F	R^2
	0.1064	0.024	−0.002	8.374*	0.0049
	15.89*	3.551*	−1.968**		

Model 3: Cash flow based

Intercept	RCF$_t$	RCE$_{t-1}$	F	R^2
Coefficient	0.110	0.004	−0.0004	3.106**	0.0017
t	13.99**	2.456*	−0.434		

RCE = Relative change in earnings: RNVA = relative change in net value added; RCF = relative change in cash flows.
Significant at *α = 0.01; **α = 0.05; and ***α = 0.10.

Source: Riahi-Belkaoui, Ahmed, "The Information Content of Value Added, Earnings and Cash Flows: U.S. Evidence," *The International Journal of Accounting* 28 (1993): 143. Reprinted with permission.

Results

Exhibits 3.5 and 3.6 present, respectively, the results of the regression on simple and combined return effects. The six equations are significant at p = 0.05. Each of the measures of accounting return, value added, income, or cash flows is significant in explaining the changes in security returns. The tests for relative and incremental information content are shown, respectively, in Exhibits 3.7 and 3.8.

Exhibit 3.7 presents the levels of significance for the relative information content comparisons. For the pooled sample and the period examined, value added exhibits greater relative information content than net income and cash flows ($p < 0.01$), and net income exhibits greater relative information content than cash flows ($p < 0.03$).

Exhibit 3.6
Regression Results on Combined Return Effects

Model 4: Earnings and Net Value Added

	Intercept	RCE_t	RCE_{t-1}	$RNVA_t$	$RNVA_{t-1}$	F	R^2
Coefficient	0.11	0.001	0.004	0.024	-0.008	6.777*	0.0025
t		15.99	2.888*	1.84**	3.527	-0.989	

Model 5: Earnings and Cash Flow Based

	Intercept	RCE_t	RCE_{t-1}	$RNVA_t$	$RNVA_{t-1}$	F	R^2
Coefficient	0.11	0.0016	0.0051	-0.002		4.26*	0.0047
t		14.22*	0.45*	2.106**	2.56*	-1.816**	

Model 6: Value Added and Cash Flow Based

	Intercept	RCE_t	RCE_{t-1}	$RNVA_t$	$RNVA_{t-1}$	F	R^2
Coefficient	0.108	0.023	-0.0003	0.0034	-0.0009	5.593*	0.0067
t		16.01*	3.46*	-2.47*	2.56*	-0.53	

Significant at *$\alpha = 0.01$; **$\alpha = 0.05$; and ***$\alpha = 0.10$.

Source: Riahi-Belkaoui, Ahmed, "The Information Content of Value Added, Earnings and Cash Flows: U.S. Evidence," *The International Journal of Accounting* 28 (1993): 143. Reprinted with permission.

Exhibit 3.8 presents the results for tests of incremental information content. It also shows the information content of value added to be dominating, exhibiting incremental information content beyond both net income and cash flows. Similarly, net income dominates cash flows.

Exhibit 3.7
Tests for Relative Information Content for Net Income, Cash Flows, and Value Added

Ranking	Value added	>	Net income	>	Cash flows
Adjusted R^2	0.0049	>	0.0019	>	0.0017
p-value		.01		.03	

Source: Riahi-Belkaoui, Ahmed, "The Information Content of Value Added, Earnings and Cash Flows: U.S. Evidence," *The International Journal of Accounting* 28 (1993): 144. Reprinted with permission.

MERITS OF DERIVED ACCOUNTING INDICATOR NUMBERS

Objectives

The main objective of this chapter is to address the usefulness issue of accrual accounting, cash flow accounting, and value added reporting by an evaluation of the relative merits of accounting indicators derived from each of the three accounting systems. The indicators have two basic characteristics. First, they are computed as per share numbers and, second, they are ratios whose denominator is the market price of a share. The first characteristic is intended to ensure comparability between the indicators and the firms. The second characteristic is to ensure that the indicator reflects a rate of return on a market investment.

First, the cash flow per share/stock price of security i for time period t, $CFP_{i,t}$, is defined as

$$CFP_{i,t} = (CFO_{i,t}/CSO_{i,t})/P_{i,t}$$

where

$P_{i,t}$ = price of a security i at the end of period t adjusted for capital changes such as stock splits and stock dividends;

$CFO_{i,t}$ = cash flows generated from continuing operations, where cash flows are defined as income available to common depreciation, deferred taxes, and the changes in noncash working capital; and

Exhibit 3.8
Incremental Comparison

1. Information content (value added /income)	= information content (value added, income) information content (income) = 0.0025 − 0.0019 = 0.006
2. Information content (value added/cash flows)	= information content (value added, cash flows) information content (cash flows) = 0.0067 − 0.0017 = 0.005
3. Information content (cash flows/value added)	= information content (cash flows, income) information content (income) = 0.0067 − 0.0049 = 0.0024
4. Information content (cash flows/ income)	= Information content (cash flows, income) information content (income) = 0.0067 − 0.0019 = 0.0048
5. Information content (cash flows/income)	= information content (cash flows, income) information content (income) = 0.0067 − 0.0019 = 0.0048
6. Information content (income/cash flow)	= information content (income, cash flow) information content (cash flows) = 0.0067 − 0.0017 = 0.0050

Source: Riahi-Belkaoui, Ahmed, "The Information Content of Value Added, Earnings and Cash Flows: U.S. Evidence," *The International Journal of Accounting* 28 (1993): 144. Reprinted with permission.

$CSO_{i,t}$ = common shares outstanding of firm i in periods t.

Second, the earning per share/stock price of security i for time period t, $EPSP_{i,t}$, is defined as follows:

$$EPSP_{i,t} = EPS_{i,t}/P_{i,t}$$

where

$EPS_{i,t}$ = income available to common equity.

Third, the net value added per share/stock price of security i for time period t, $NVAP_{i,t}$, is defined as follows:

$$NVAP_{i,t} = (NVA_{i,t}/CSO_{i,t})/P_{i,t}$$

where

$NVA_{i,t}$ = net value added computed as the sum of labor expenses, corporate taxes, dividends, interest expense, minority shareholders in subsidiaries, and retained earnings.

Each of these numbers, $CFP_{i,t}$, $EPSP_{i,t}$, and $NVA_{i,t}$, represents numbers derived from cash flow accounting, accrual accounting, or value added reporting, and related to stock price, and whose merits will be evaluated in terms of variability and persistence. These numbers represent semi-accounting indices of rate of return derived from cash flow accounting, accrual accounting, or value added reporting.[6]

The Sample Design

A single criterion was used for the selection of firms to be included in the sample. The accounting and market variables needed to compute each of the three semi-accounting indices of rate of return were available on Compustat. Six hundred seventy-three companies representing 23 industries met the sampling requirement.

Three semi-accounting indices of rate of return were used for a comparison of the relative merits of accrual, cash flow, and value added reporting:

1. A cash flow per share/stock price ratio was used to represent the cash flow accounting–derived semi-accounting index of rate of return.
2. An earnings per share/stock price ratio was used to represent the accrual accounting–derived and income statement–oriented semi-accounting index of rate of return.
3. A net value added per share/stock price ratio was used to represent the value added reporting–derived semi-accounting index of rate of return.

Results

Variability of Derived Accounting Indicator Numbers

The semi-accounting rates of return, $CFP_{i,t}$, $EPSP_{i,t}$, and $NVAP_{i,t}$, were computed for the 673 firms for the years 1981–1990. The statistical properties of the three distributions are shown in Exhibit 3.9. From Exhibit 3.9 we can see that the mean rate of return based on net value added

Exhibit 3.9
Statistical Properties of Derived Accounting Indicators

	NVAP	CFP	EPSP
Observations	4993	5649	5609
Mean	1.661	0.14809	0.03142
Standard Deviation	2.04426	1.0791	0.49566
Skewness	15.9524	34.8725	-10.8074
Coefficient of Variation	175.3305	728.7165	1577.403
Kurtosis	386.7382	1678.171	151.4351
Maximum	69.119	57.334	3.783
Minimum	0.003	-9.338	-9.327
Range	69.116	66.672	13.11

Source: Riahi-Belkaoui, Ahmed, and M. Ali Fekrat, "The Magic of Value Added: Merits of Derived Accounting Indicator Numbers," *Managerial Finance* 20, no. 9 (1994): 12. Reprinted with permission.

ranges from a high of 69.119 to a low of 0.003. The mean rate of return based in net value added amounts to NVAP = 1.1661. The mean rate of return based on cash flows ranges from a high of 57.334 to a low of −9.338. The mean rate of return based on cash flows amounts to CFP = 0.14809. The mean rate of return based on earnings ranges from a high of 3.783 to a low of −9.327. The mean rate of return based on earnings amounts to EPSP = 0.03142. In all of the 673 cases examined, the NVAP exceeded both EPSP and CFP.

The differences in variability, which are the focus of this section, are illustrated by the coefficient of variation. From Exhibit 3.9 we can see that the coefficient of variation of NVAP is drastically lower than the coefficient of variation of both EPSP and CFP. The same result was found for all the 673 cases examined.

It is interesting to speculate why the variability of the net value added rate of return is lower than the earnings rate of return and the cash flow–based rates of return. To begin with, all three semi-accounting rates of return have as their denominator the market price of a share of common stock. The variability of the latter is the same for all three measures of rates of return. Consequently, differences in variability among NVAP, CFP, and EPSP must be attributed to the variability of the numerators, that is, net value added per share, cash flow per share, and accrual earnings per share. Why then would net value added be subject to less variability than cash flow or accrual earnings? The reason seems to lie mainly in the way these numbers are defined and constructed. Generally, when a number such as accrual earnings is derived as a residual from a process in which some of the intervening numbers, such as depreciation, interest, or wages, are fixed or ''sticky,'' a given change in a variable such as sales revenue will be accompanied by a more than proportionate change in the residual. The residual is further affected by many allocation, valuation, and classification decisions. It is precisely because of the latter and because the derivation of accrual earnings and cash flow involve a larger number of intervening variables than does the derivation of net value added and because of leads and lags in these variables that accrual earnings and cash flow data show greater variability. Discretionary income smoothing practices are of minor importance[7] because the observed effect of smoothing on earnings is the result of all accounting practices.[8] The evidence here suggests that smoothing, whether due to changes in accounting methods or changes in the timing of investments/production/financing activities, is probably not at work. Income smoothing exists if the ratio of the coefficient of variation of accrual earnings to the coefficient of variation in sales revenue is less than unity. Using value added as a rough surrogate for sales revenue, the ratios for both accrual earnings and cash flows based on Exhibit 3.9 data are about 4 and 9. This implies that of the three semi-accounting rates of return, the value added–based return efficiently reflects the market as it is unencumbered by the variability caused by built-in allocation, valuation, and classification decisions and various other intervening variables.

Persistency of Derived Accounting Indicator Numbers

The persistency of the derived accounting indicator numbers was determined by examining the median rank correlation between the accounting indicator number in the year of formation and the same number in subsequent years. A similar methodology was used by Beaver and Morse[9] and Bildersee, Cheh, and Lee.[10] Exhibits 3.10, 3.11, and 3.12 show consecutively the rank correlation of all the sample companies' NVAP, EPSP, and CFP with the NVAP, EPSP, and CFP in subsequent years. The median correlation of each column is reported at the bottom of the tables.

The median correlation of NVAP numbers shown in Exhibit 3.10 decreased from 0.894 in the first year after formation to 0.745 in the ninth year after formation. Five years after formation the median correlation is 0.74132.

The median correlation of EPSP numbers shown in Exhibit 3.11 decreases from 0.623 in the first year after formation to 0.192 in the ninth year after formation. Five years after formation the median correlation is 0.508.

The median correlation of CFP numbers shown in Exhibit 3.12 decreases from 0.689 in the first year after formation to 0.402 in the ninth year after formation. Five years after formation the median correlation is 0.508.

The results support a long-term persistency in the NVAP numbers and low persistency in the EPSP and CFP numbers. The same reasons given to explain the lower variability of NVAPs compared to EPSPs and CFPs apply to the persistency results.

The results of this section indicate that derived accounting indicator numbers based on net value added had low variability and higher persistency than corresponding numbers based on either earnings or cash flows of 673 U.S. firms for the 1981–1990 period. The result is mainly due to the absence of smoothing of the total return earned by a firm and computed by the value added figure. The market is efficiently reflecting

Exhibit 3.10
Rank Correlation of All the Sample Companies: NVAPs with NVAPs in Subsequent Years

Base Year	Years Following Base Year									
	1	2	3	4	5	6	7	8	9	10
1990	0.91282	0.88300	0.82872	0.78669	0.75946	0.75190	0.72466	0.72907	0.74480	
1989	0.90142	0.84565	0.79889	0.76604	0.76095	0.71512	0.71316	074272		
1988	0.90170	0.87385	0.83027	0.79411	0.72674	0.71312	0.74510			
1987	0.89634	0.82309	0.78605	0.72730	0.68940	0.73233				
1986	0.87710	0.82646	0.76053	0.72152	0.74132					
1985	0.88453	0.81710	0.78108	0.79111						
1984	0.89412	0.84931	0.85225							
1983	0.91417	0.8934								
1982	0.926023									
1981										
	0.89412	0.81137	0.79885	0.77636	0.74132	0.72672	0.72466	0.73589	0.74480	

Source: Riahi-Belkaoui, Ahmed, and M. Ali Fekrat, "The Magic of Value Added: Merits of Derived Accounting Indicator Numbers," *Managerial Finance* 20, no. 9 (1994): 13. Reprinted with permission.

Exhibit 3.11
Rank Correlation of All Sample Companies: EPSPs with EPSPs in Subsequent Years

Base Year	S	2	3	4	5	6	7	8	9
1990	0.41232	0.31394	0.20400	0.23430	0.23137	0.19289	0.23453	0.27798	0.19243
1989	0.51261	0.36660	0.21002	0.17728	0.22298	0.23793	0.21098		
1988	0.40461	0.42216	0.31923	0.36821	0.36968	0.25143	0.28483		
1987	0.46408	0.34827	0.62199	0.34923	0.16746	0.18474			
1986	0.64904	0.52507	0.50614	0.49261	0.38066				
1985	0.65594	0.67292	0.48701	0.35107					
1984	0.73561	0.55707							
1983	0.73505	0.51948							
1982	0.62282								
1981									
Median Correlation	0.62282	0.47361	0.38380	0.35015	0.23137	0.21541	0.23453	0.25012	0.19243

Source: Riahi-Belkaoui, Ahmed, and M. Ali Fekrat, "The Magic of Value Added: Merits of Derived Accounting Indicator Numbers," *Managerial Finance* 20, no. 9 (1994): 14. Reprinted with permission.

Exhibit 3.12
Rank Correlation of All Sample Companies: CFPs with CFPs in Subsequent Years

Base Year	S	2	3	4	5	6	7	8	9
1990	0.47972	0.48477	0.95469	0.46547	0.47029	0.48547	0.41618	0.40170	0.40150
1989	0.60084	0.56530	0.44610	0.47148	0.50811	0.44379	0.43642	0.53544	
1988	0.61172	0.66970	0.59829	0.59993	0.55225	0.45883	0.55074		
1987	0.64771	0.56053	0.58910	0.51530	0.47091	0.56083			
1986	0.68863	0.69400	0.64974	0.55286	0.60716				
1985	0.77178	0.74345	0.61717	0.58747					
1984	0.78394	0.72690	0.72752						
1983	0.80538	0.72941							
1982	0.74034								
1981									
Median Correlation	0.68863	0.68185	0.59829	0.53408	0.50811	0.47215	0.43642	0.46857	0.40150

Source: Riahi-Belkaoui, Ahmed, and M. Ali Fekrat, "The Magic of Value Added: Merits of Derived Accounting Indicator Numbers," *Managerial Finance* 20, no. 9 (1994): 15. Reprinted with permission.

this total return and generating the lower variability and higher persistency of the value added–based performance indicator number of U.S. firms used in this study.

The ultimate test of any new accounting information is, of course, its usefulness, both in terms of the relationship of the new data to stock prices and in terms of managerial decision-making usefulness. How does the value added information stand up to the test? In terms of stock prices, evidence suggests that at least at the firm level, the accounting measures of risk based on value added data have a much greater association with the market measures of risk than do accrual earnings or cash flows.

NONLINEAR SPECIFICATION

Recent studies examining the functional specification relating unexpected earnings to market-adjusted returns suggest the existence of non-linearities in the relationship.[11, 12] This section differs on two counts. First, in addition to earnings, a known and conventional measure of accounting return, it examines net value added, a measure of wealth created and attributable to all stakeholders and advocated as an important European innovation worthy of inclusion in U.S. company annual reports. Second, this study uses raw returns as variables in the analysis rather than expected returns.

Rationale

The main advantage of the value added approach is in its ability to measure the total wealth created by the company before distribution to the various stakeholders. As such it contains information beyond traditional "bottom line" earnings that is useful in explaining the behavior of share prices.

Three arguments can be used to support the thesis that shareholders would be interested in the total wealth created in the company.

First, the expectation that the "value added" variable contains more value-relevant information than the "earnings" variable approach is based on prior research that indicates (a) additional disclosure released concurrently with announcements of annual earnings has information content beyond that contained in earnings per se and (b) components of earnings explain more of the variation in returns than is explained by earnings alone.

Second, although shareholders are interested in their share of the total wealth created, their primary concerns involve (a) a knowledge of what is the total wealth created and (b) how it is going to be apportioned over time. Shareholders are basically competing with other members of the "team" (i.e., government, labor, and bondholders) for the distribution of total wealth. The higher the total wealth and the lower (or unchanged) the portion allocated to government, labor, and bondholders, the higher the profit accruing to shareholders.

Third, accounting earnings are plagued with measurement and management problems that may hinder explanatory and predictive abilities. Value added was found to possess incremental information beyond both accrual earnings and cash flows in the context of explaining market risk. Similarly, takeover targets have lower value added to total asset ratios (both mean and median) than the average in their industries in the year preceding the resolution of the takeover. In both contexts of prediction of systematic risk and takeover, earning variables explain less than value added variables.

In sum, the "value added" variable—which is computed by the addition to earnings of other components of earnings—explains more of the variation in returns than is explained by earnings alone.

Thus the basic question is whether the more comprehensive disclosure of value added variables will contain information relevant to the pricing of securities. This question can be addressed by examining potential nonlinearities with regard to the functional specification relating both earnings and net value added to market returns, as well as the explanatory ability of a nonlinear model based on either earnings or net value added.

The examination of nonlinearity rests on two arguments. First, the time relation between market-adjusted returns and accounting returns is unobservable. Second, some empirical evidence suggests that the relation is not constant. For example, Chambers and Penman[13] and Hughes and Ricks[14] examined the timeliness of earnings announcement and indicated that the stock price reaction is greater for early versus late disclosures. A study of a sample of initial offerings suggested that the relation varied as investors learn about the earnings process of firms.[15] The stock price reaction to earnings announcements is also found to be symmetric for good and bad news, suggesting that the relation changes as a function of the sign of the earnings surprise.[16] Finally, nonlinearities have been detected in at least two studies.[17, 18]

Valuation Models

Linear Models

A typical "linear" valuation model rests on expressing a relationship between relative changes in price and earnings.[19, 20] One formulation of this model can be expressed as:

$$(P_{jt} + d_{jt})/P_{jt-1} = a_{1jt} + a_{2jt}(A_{jt}/A_{jt-1}) + a_{3jt}SIZE_{jt} + a_{4jt}LEV_{jt}$$
$$+ a_{5jt}MB + e_{2jt} \tag{11}$$

where

P_{jt} = market price of security j,

d_{jt} = dividend,

A_{jt} = accounting earnings,

$SIZE_{jt}$ = natural logarithm of assets,

LEV_{jt} = long-term debt over total assets, and

MB_{jt} = ratio of market to book value.

This model suggests there is a relationship between the relative change in security prices and the relative changes in earnings. Three additional conditional variables are added to help explain the relative change in return given a certain level of earnings change: (1) the natural logarithm of assets (SIZE), (2) the ratio of long-term debt to assets (LEV), and (3) the ratio of market to book value (MB). These three variables are added to proxy for risk, size effects in the measurement of changes in returns, and growth or persistence, respectively.

Given the arguments used earlier—that net value added contains informational content that is relevant to the pricing of securities—a second linear model is also investigated:

$$(P_{jt} + d_{jt})/P_{jt-1} = a_{1jt} + a_{2jt}(NVA_{jt}/NVA_{jt-1}) + a_{3jt}SIZE_{jt}$$
$$+ a_{4jt}LEV_{jt} + a_{5jt}MB_{jt} + e_{3jt} \tag{12}$$

where

NVA = net value added.

This model suggests there is a relationship between the relative change in security prices and the relative changes in net value added. The three conditioning variables of SIZE, LEV, and MB are also included in this model.

Nonlinear Models

Both equations (11) and (12) express the relationship between market and accounting returns found in the conventional linear model. Alternative nonlinear models can be proposed to test the potential nonlinear specification of the relationship.

The convex-concave form ("S-shaped" or an "S-curve") is proposed as the nonlinear expression of the relationship between market returns and accounting returns, measured by either earnings or net value added. The relationship between accounting earnings—as measured by either earnings or net value added—and market returns has a positive first derivative. It is convex for bad news and is concave for good news, that is, a convex-concave relationship between accounting and market returns. This convex-concave relationship is based on prior findings that (a) the ratio of permanent to transitory earnings declines as the absolute magnitude of unexpected earnings increases and (b) the transitory earnings surprises have significantly less impact on security prices than permanent earnings surprises.[21, 22]

Accordingly, the nonlinear specification used in this study is a quadratic function where the quadratic term is allowed to depend on the sign of the relative change in either earnings or net value added. It is expressed as follows:

$$(P_{jt} + d_{jt})/P_{jt-1} = b_{1jt} + b_{2jt}(A_{jt}/A_{jt-1}) + b_{3jt}D(A_{jt}/A_{jt-1})^2$$
$$+ b_{4jt}SIZE_{jt} + b_{5jt}LEV_{jt} + b_{6jt}MB_{jt} + e_{4jt} \quad (13)$$

$$(P_{jt} + d_{jt})/P_{jt-1} = b'_{1jt} + b'_{2jt}(NVA_{jt}/NVA_{jt-1})$$
$$+ b'_{3jt}D(NVA_{jt}/NVA_{jt-1})^2$$
$$+ b'_{4jt}SIZE_{jt} + b'_{5jt}LEV_{jt} + b'_{6jt}MB_{jt} + e_{5jt} \quad (14)$$

Here D is an indicator variable taking a value of 1 when the relative change in either earnings or net value added is positive and -1 when the change is negative, thereby producing a convex-concave function. The prediction is that both b_{3t} and b_{3t}' will be negative based on the thesis that investors' perceptions of the persistence of the surprise are negatively correlated with its magnitude.

Data and Sample Selection

The analysis focuses on security return and its relationship to either earnings or net value added. Security returns (R_{jt}) for security j in year t were defined as the security price at the end of the year plus cash dividends divided by security price at the beginning of the year. The use of R_{jt} rather than some form of residual returns follows from findings of prior studies that the correlation between security returns and earnings is essentially the same under either form of the security return metric.

The accounting return variables used were either based on accounting earnings or net value added. They were defined from Compustat items as follows:

1. Net value added (NVA) = the sum of labor expenses, corporate taxes, interest expenses, minority shareholders in subsidiaries, and retained earnings.
2. Earnings (A) = Income available to common equity.

Each variable was defined using Compustat's annual industrial data definition as follows:

$$NVA = (42_t + 6_t + 19_t + 21_t + 15_t + 49_t + 36_t - 36_{t-1}) \text{ and}$$
$$A = (20_t).$$

The firms examined in this study represented all NYSE and AMEX firms that had available NVA, A, and R data over the period 1981–1990 in Compustat. The selection procedure resulted in 4,660 firm-year observations after deleting 132 firm-year observations. The deletion affected those cases where A_{jt}/P_{t-1} is not between $+1.5$ and -1.5. This truncation rule was imposed to ensure that the results were not unduly affected by a few outlying (unusual) observations. However, the truncation did not change the substance of the results.

Results

Three important results emerged. First the net value added–returns relationships offer slightly more explanatory power than the earnings-returns relationships when the relationships are expressed by a linear model. Regressions results on linear models are presented in Exhibit 3.13. Panel A includes the cross-sectional regressions, whereas panel B includes the pooled cross-sectional time-series regressions. The adjusted R^2 for nine of the ten cases in panel A and the six cases in panel B is slightly higher for the net value added data–based linear model than the earnings-based linear model. The coefficient of earnings (a_2) is significant for seven out of ten cases in panel A and five out of six cases in panel B. The influence of the conditioning variables is significant, particularly for SIZE and MB in most cases.

Second, the net value added–based returns relationships still offer better explanatory power than the earnings-returns relationships, when the relationships are expressed by a nonlinear, convex-concave function. In addition, the convex-concave function is more pronounced in the net value added than the earnings-based functions and cases. Regression results on nonlinear models are presented in Exhibit 3.14. Panel A includes the cross-sectional regressions, whereas panel B includes the pooled cross-sectional time series regressions. In each case, the adjusted R^2 for the ten cases in panel A and the six cases in panel B is slightly higher for the value added–based nonlinear model than the earnings-based nonlinear models. The convex-concave function, stipulating that b_3 or b_3' will be significant and negative is verified for all the cases in panels A and B for the net value added–based nonlinear models. It is verified for only some cases for the earnings-based nonlinear models.

Finally, comparison of the results presented in Exhibits 3.13 and 3.14 for all the cases shows that in general (a) the nonlinear models have better explanatory power than the linear models and (b) the net value added–based nonlinear models have the best explanatory power.

CONCLUSIONS

The use of value added reporting is on the increase worldwide. Calls have been made for its adoption by domestic corporations. The results of this chapter make a favorable case for the adoption of value added reporting in the United States. The models relating accounting and market returns have more explanatory power when (a) the accounting returns are expressed by the relative changes in net value added and (b) the relationship is a nonlinear, convex-concave function.

The important policy implication of this chapter is that the value added accounting information can supply additional explanatory power of mar-

Exhibit 3.13
Linear Regression Results

Cross-Sectional Regressions

Panel A

<u>Based on Earnings</u>

Year	N	a1	a2	a3	a4	a5	R2	F
1990	480	-0.2830*	0.0070*	0.0070	0.3780*	-0.0006	0.2042	32.440'
		-5.2010	4.1400	1.1670	4.7670	-9.0120		
1989	499	0.2660	0.0030	-0.0130***	0.0710	-0.0002*	0.0290	3.7690'
		3.8200	0.4470	-1.6080	0.7030	-3.2660		
1988	484	-0.2070	-0.0020	0.0850	-0.8900	0.0040	0.0340	0.7260'
		-0.3440	-0.1880	1.2020	-1.0060	-0.3910		
1987	473	-0.0500	0.0140*	-0.0080	0.1280	-0.0010*	0.0452	7.4240'
		-0.6270	2.7520	-0.9040	1.0850	-3.9720		
1986	462	-0.0115	0.0040	0.0110	0.8240*	-0.0050*	0.1307	17.410'
		-1.1960	0.8600	0.9210	5.9620	-2.9650		
1985	478	0.2533*	0.0250*	0.0020	0.0260	0.0020	0.0040	1.5120
		3.1580	2.0050	0.2570	0.2410	1.1070		
1984	477	-0.1950	0.0460*	0.0270*	0.1610**	0.0010	0.0517	10.029'
		3.3470	4.4670	3.5430	1.9960	-1.0070		
1983	448	0.1340	0.0550*	0.0110	-0.1610	0.0020	0.0397	10.260
		1.3030	5.7940	0.8930	-1.1770	1.3260		
1982	431	0.3490*	0.0760*	-0.0080	0.2360**	-0.0040*	0.0700	10.350'
		3.7790	4.4930	-0.7260	1.9320	-2.8760		
1981	418	0.0770	0.0390*	-0.0140	0.3880*	0.0040*	0.1103	7.2900'
		0.9500	3.1400	-1.3450	3.6480	2.9720		

Exhibit 3.13 (Continued)

Cross-Sectional Regressions

Panel A

Based on Net Value Added

Year	N	a1'	a2'	a3'	a4'	a5'	R2	F
1990	480	-0.287*	0.0360*	0.0060	0.3870*	-0.0006*	0.2142	30.53*
		-5.2290	3.3060	1.0390	4.8610	-8.9480		
1989	499	0.2700	0.0000	-0.0130***	0.0600	0.0002*	0.0291	3.73*
		3.8960	0.2260	-1.6890	0.6890	-3.2520		
1988	484	-0.3500	-0.201 *	0.1060***	-0.9450	-0.0005	0.0660	4.34*
		-0.6060	-3.7970	1.5150	-1.0850	0.4820		
1987	473	-0.0390	0.0086*	-0.0103	0.1330	-0.0010*	0.0595	5.547*
		-0.4840	0.6330	-1.0620	1.1170	-3.9900		
1986	462	-0.1210	-0.0040	0.0120	0.8090*	-0.0060*	0.1320	17.212*
		-1.2540	-0.2160	1.0700	5.8990	-4.2550		
1985	478	0.2490	0.0010*	0.0030	0.0040	0.0020	0.0120	0.506*
		3.0910	0.1220	0.3140	0.0420	1.1470		
1984	477	-0.220 *	0.0990*	0.0300*	0.1560**	-0.0020**	0.0782	6.422*
		-3.6910	2.4850	3.9120	1.8960	-2.2660		
1983	448	0.1110	0.1800*	0.0190	-0.299 **	-0.0003	0.0840	4.595
		1.0490	3.3520	1.4110	-2.1440	-0.1840		
1982	431	0.3820*	0.1880*	-0.0130	0.1360	-0.0040*	0.0880	8.134
		4.1180	3.4230	-1.1180	1.0950	-2.6610		
1981	418	0.0390	0.3620*	-0.0150***	0.4040*	0.0010	0.0650	12.831*
		0.4920	5.570	-1.4970	3.9130	1.4650		

58

Exhibit 3.13 (Continued)

Pooled Cross-Sectional Time Series Regressions

Panel B

<u>Based on Earnings</u>

Range of

Relative Change

in Return (RCR)	N	a1	a2	a3	a4	a5	R2	
¦RCR¦ <	4660	0.036	0.0068**	0.007	0.137	−0.0040*	0.0030	4.14
		0.513	1.9750	0.894	1.415	−3.1220		
¦RCR¦ < .1	2317	−0.236*	0.0070*	0.007*	0.070*	−0.0003*	0.0701	46.30
		−11.987	7.4330	3.055	2.394	−10.7360		
¦RCR¦ < .05	2032	−0.255*	0.0070*	0.005*	0.027	−0.0003*	0.0762	41.79
		−12.789	7.0810	2.465	0.517	−10.5310		
¦RCR¦ < .01	1811	−0.295*	0.0070*	0.007*	0.033	−0.0002*	0.0823	40.78
		−14.646	6.9570	2.957	1.095	−10.3070		
¦RCR¦ < .005	1790	−0.295*	0.0070*	0.006*	0.030	−0.0020*	0.0821	40.29
		−14.617	6.9440	2.805	1.007	−10.2650		
¦RCR¦ < .001	1770	−0.292*	0.0060*	0.006*	0.030	−0.0002*	0.0818	39.39
		−14.426	6.8560	2.463	0.978	−10.2260		

Exhibit 3.13(Continued)

Pooled Cross-Sectional Time Series Regressions

Panel B

Based on Net Value Added

Range of Relative Change in Return (RCR)	N	a1′	a2′	a3′	a4′	a5′	R2	F
¦RCR¦ <	4660	0.037	0.000	0.007	0.137	-0.0004*	0.0031	3.19*
		0.521	-0.319	0.871	1.414	-3.1630		
¦RCR¦ < .1	2317	-0.239*	0.013*	0.007*	0.007*	-0.0030*	0.0767	34.70*
		-12.003	3.337	2.928	2.379	-9.8550		
¦RCR¦ < .05	2032	-0.257*	0.013*	0.005**	0.028	-0.0002*	0.0785	31.40*
		-12.762	3.335	2.294	0.935	-9.6360		
¦RCR¦ < .01	1811	-0.298*	0.011*	0.006*	0.035	-0.0002*	0.0832	29.97*
		-14.830	2.775	2.818	1.164	-9.4250		
¦RCR¦ < .005	1790	-0.298*	0.011*	0.006*	0.033	-0.0002*	0.0829	29.47*
		-14.586	2.730	2.673	1.084	-9.3910		
¦RCR¦ < .001	1770	-0.294*	0.010*	0.005*	0.033	-0.0002*	0.0829	28.64*
		-14.397	2.543	2.335	1.078	-9.3750		

*Significant at $\alpha = 0.01$.
**Significant at $\alpha = 0.05$.
***Significant at $\alpha = 0.10$.

The test statistics are t statistics because White's (1980) test for heteroskedasticity in the residuals revealed no significant heteroskedasticity. When there is (is not) significant heteroskedasticity, the test statistic reported for the intercepts and the slopes cue the z statistics (t statistics) appropriate for such cases.

Exhibit 3.14
Nonlinear Regression Results

Cross-Sectional Regressions

Panel A

Based on Earnings

Year	N	a1	a2	a3	a4	a5	a6	R2	F
1990	480	-0.285	0.014	-0.0001**	0.007	0.381*	-0.006*	0.2185	26.55
		-5.236	3.254	-1.601	1.204	4.818	-9.107		
1989	499	0.285	0.015	0.001*	-0.011	0.066	-0.002*	0.0503	5.232
		3.743	1.892	3.285	-1.459	0.663	-3.116		
1988	484	-0.217	-0.01	0	0.086	-0.892	-0.004	0.006	0.592
		-0.36	-0.31	-0.248	1.218	-1.007	-0.385		
1987	473	-0.071	0.033	-0.0007*	-0.005	0.1504	-0.001*	0.079	8.08
		-0.891	4.229	-3.189	-0.592	1.285	-4.024		
1986	462	-0.11	0.018	-0.002**	0.011	0.827*	-0.005*	0.1326	14.47
		-1.147	1.799	-1.538	0.927	5.99	-3.11		
1985	478	0.253	0.025	0.0004	0.002	0.026	0.002	0.012	1.227
		3.153	2.021	0.306	0.249	0.241	1.125		
1984	477	-0.192	0.079	-0.005*	0.027	0.147**	-0.001	0.098	10.32
		-3.33	5.507	-3.27	3.661	1.838	-1.405		
1983	448	-0.109	0.137	-0.003*	0.013	-0.166	0.004**	0.1343	13.74
		1.088	7.362	-5.04	1.019	-1.251	2.115		
1982	431	0.348	0.075	0.006	-0.008	0.238**	-0.004*	0.0886	8.282
		3.751	4.337	0.298	-0.716	1.943	-2.822		
1981	418	-0.075	0.038	0.001	-0.013	0.377*	0.003*	0.0681	6.033
		0.922	2.955	0.985	-1.277	3.521	2.811		

61

Exhibit 3.14 (Continued)

Cross-Sectional Regressions

Panel A

Based on Net Value Added

Year	N	a1'	a2'	a3'	a4'	a5'	a6'	R2	F
1990	480	-0.277	0.156*	-0.013*	0.003	0.003	-0.0006*	0.2563	32.73
		-5.203	6.69	-5.767	0.65	4.373	-8.485		
1989	499	0.279	0.023*	0 *	-0.01 **	0.079	-0.0001*	0.057	6.06
		4.081	3.874	-0.867	-1.943	0.795	-2.44		
1988	484	-0.17	-1.04 *	0.022*	0.101	-1.13	-0.001 *	0.1228	13.4
		-0.307	-2.925	6.925	1.518	-1.365	-0.903		
1987	473	-0.079	0.132*	-0.008*	-0.007	0.172	-0.001 *	0.0731	7.385
		-0.985	3.72	-3.757	-0.805	1.966	-3.41		
1986	462	-0.137	0.064**	-0.006**	0.013	0.842*	-0.005 *	0.1362	14.41
		-1.417	1.463	-1.715	1.113	6.092	-3.975		
1985	478	0.222	0.152*	-0.008*	0.001	0.13	0.003	0.0381	3.74
		2.794	3.817	-4.071	0.176	1.137	1.563		
1984	477	-0.23	0.23 *	-0.098**	0.292*	0.171**	-0.002 **	0.059	6.17
		-3.852	3.041	-2.036	3.82	2.082	-2.256		
1983	448	0.094	0.34 *	-0.04 **	0.018	-0.294**	0.0009	0.149	4.567
		0.895	3.628	-2.079	1.39	-2.12	0.421		
1982	431	0.366	0.449*	-0.104*	-0.012	0.124	-0.004 *	0.091	8.54
		3.979	4.466	-3.085	-1.407	1.011	-2.779		
1981	418	0.037	0.413	-0.056	-0.015	1.404*	0.001	0.1109	10.304
		0.461	3.58	-0.535	-1.522	3.911	1.393		

Exhibit 3.14 (Continued)

Nonlinear Regressions

Pooled Cross-Sectional Time Series Regressions

Panel B

<u>Based on Earnings</u>

Range of Relative

Change In Return	N	c1	c2	c3	c4	c5	c6	R2	F
$\lvert RCR \rvert$ <	4659	0.039	0.011	0.000**	0.007	0.132	-0.0004	0.004	4.2
		0.549	2.783	2.128	0.871	1.363	-3.091		
$\lvert RCR \rvert$ < .1	2317	-0.237	0.01	-0.000	0.007	0.07	-0.0003	0.075	37.
		-12.009	5.051	-1.349	3.099	2.431	-10.788		
$\lvert RCR \rvert$ < .05	2032	-0.255	0.009	-3E-05	0.006	0.028	-0.0003	0.076	33.
		-12.802	4.54	-0.962	2.497	0.946	-10.564		
$\lvert RCR \rvert$ < .01	1811	-0.296	0.086	0	0.007	0.034	-0.0002	0.083	32.
		-14.658	4.37	-0.889	2.987	1.125	-10.327		
$\lvert RCR \rvert$ < .005	1790	-0.296	0.008	0	0.006	0.031	-0.0002	0.083	32.
		-14.628	4.339	-0.864	2.833	1.035	-10.294		
$\lvert RCR \rvert$ < .001	1770	-0.292	0.008	0	0.006	0.03	-0.0002	0.082	31.
		-14.436	4.205	-0.78	2.792	1.003	-10.251		

Exhibit 3.14 (Continued)

Nonlinear Regressions

Pooled Cross-Sectional Time Series Regressions

Panel B

<u>Based on Net Value Added</u>

Range of Relative

Change In Return	N	c1'	c2'	c3'	c4'	c5'	c6'	R2	F
|RCR| <	4659	0.03	-0.05	4E-05*	0.009	0.138	-0.005	0.005	7.22
		0.043	-4.829	4.819	1.057	1.495	-3.628		
|RCR| < .1	2317	-0.247	0.07	0.000**	0.007	0.094*	-0.000	0.085	38.2
		-12.51	7.764	-6.997	3.006	3.819	-9.164		
|RCR| < .05	2032	-0.265	0.066	-0.004*	0.005	0.055*	-0.000	0.086	34.7
		-13.28	7.489	-6.687	2.386	1.823	-8.927		
|RCR| < .01	1811	-0.306	0.065	-0.003*	0.007	0.063*	-0.000	0.091	33.6
		-15.14	7.254	-6.717	2.893	2.053	-8.651		
|RCR| < .005	1790	-0.305	0.64	-0.003*	0.006	0.06 **	-0.000	0.085	32.9
		-15.1	7.154	-6.63	2.75	1.962	-8.619		
|RCR| < .001	1770	-0.303	0.064	-0.003*	0.006	0.061**	-0.000	0.086	32.7
		-14.95	7.012	-6.561	2.452	1.985	-8.56		

*Significant at $\alpha = 0.01$.
**Significant at $\alpha = 0.05$.
***Significant at $\alpha = 0.10$.

The test statistics are t statistics because White's test for heteroskedasticity in the residuals revealed no significant heteroskedasticity. When there is (is not) significant heteroskedasticity, the test statistics reported for the intercepts and the slopes are the z statistics (t statistics), appropriate for such cases.

ket return beyond that provided by earnings. Thus an important accounting policy issue is whether firms should be required to disclose the underlying data needed to calculate value added variables. The current disclosure system does not mandate the disclosure of some of the information needed to compute the value added metric.

The cost of reporting this additional data should be relatively immaterial given the general availability of such information; firms already process this information for payroll purposes and when reporting such information to governmental agencies. Given the low cost relative to the potentially much greater benefit shown in this chapter, releasing value added reports or disclosing the underlying data needed to calculate the value added appears to be an improvement over the present U.S. reporting system.

NOTES

1. Easton, P. D., and T. S. Harris, "Earnings as an Explanatory Variable for Returns," *Journal of Accounting Research* (Spring 1991): 19–36.

2. Lev, B., "On the Usefulness of Earnings Research: Lessons and Directions from Two Decades of Empirical Research," *Journal of Accounting Research: Current Studies on the Informational Content of Accounting Earnings* (Supplement 1989): 153–192.

3. Lipe, R. C., "The Information Contained in the Components of Earnings," *Journal of Accounting Research* (Supplement 1986): 37–64.

4. Lev, B., "On the Usefulness of Earnings Research: Lessons and Directions from Two Decades," *Journal of Accounting Research: Current Studies on the Informational Content of Accounting Earnings* (Supplement 1989); 180.

5. The period 1979–1983 was used because it allows to generate a significantly higher number of firm-year observations than the more recent period 1988–1992. Labor-related data were more frequently disclosed in the 1978–1992 period than in other periods examined.

6. Barlev, B., and H. Levy. "On the Variability of Accounting Numbers," *Journal of Accounting Research* (Autumn 1979): 307.

7. Ibid., 306.

8. Beaver, W. H., "The Times Series Behavior of Earnings," *Journal of Accounting Research: Empirical Research in Accounting: Selected Studies* (Supplement 1970): 108.

9. Beaver, W. H., and D. Morse, "What Determines Price-Earnings Ratio," *Financial Analysts Journal* (July–August 1978): 65–76.

10. Bildersee, J. S., J. J. Cheh, and C. Lee, "The International Price-Earnings Ratio Phenomenon," *Japan and the World Economy: International Journal of Theory and Policy* 2, no. 3 (1990): 263–282.

11. Cheng, C.S.A., W. S. Hopwood, and J. C. McKeown, "Nonlinearity and Specification Problems in Unexpected Earnings Response Regression Model," *The Accounting Review* (July 1992): 579–598.

12. Freeman, R. N., and S. Y. Tse, "A Nonlinear Model of Security Price Responses to Unexpected Earnings," *Journal of Accounting Research* (Fall 1992): 157–185.

13. Chambers, A. E., and S. H. Penman, "Timeliness of Reporting and the Stock Price Reaction to Earnings Announcement," *Journal of Accounting Research* 22 (1984): 21–47.

14. Hughes, J. S., and W. E. Ricks, "Association Between Forecast Errors and Excess Returns Near to Earnings Announcements," *The Accounting Review* 62 (1987): 158–175.

15. Lang, M., "Time Varying Stock Price Responses to Earnings Induced by Uncertainty About the Time-Series Properties of Earnings," *Journal of Accounting Research* (Fall 1991): 229–260.

16. Abdel-Khalik, A. R., "Specification Problems with Information Content of Earnings: Revisions and Rationality of Expectations and Self-Selection Bias," *Contemporary Accounting Research* (Fall 1990): 142–172.

17. Beneish, M. D., and C. R. Harvey, "The Specification of the Earnings-Returns Relation," Working Paper, Duke University, August, 1993.

18. Freeman, R., J. Ohlson, and S. Penman, "Book Rate-of-Return and Predictions of Earnings Change: An Empirical Investigation," *Journal of Accounting Research* (Autumn 1982): 639–653.

19. Beaver, W., P. A. Griffin, and W. A. Landsman, "The Incremental Informational Content of Replacement Cost Earnings," *Journal of Accounting and Economics* 4 (1982): 15–39.

20. Collins, D., and S. Kothari, "A Theoretical and Empirical Analysis of the Determinants of the Relation between Earnings Innovation and Security Returns," *Journal of Accounting and Economics* (July 1989): 143–181.

21. Easton, P. D., and M. Zmijewski, "Cross-Sectional Variation in the Stock Market Response to Accounting Earnings Announcements," *Journal of Accounting and Economics* (July 1989): 117–141.

22. Kormendi, R., and R. Lipe, "Earnings Innovation, Earning Persistence, and Stock Returns," *Journal of Business* (July 1987); 37–64.

REFERENCES

Abdel-Khalik, A. R. "Specification Problems with Information Content of Earnings: Revisions and Rationality of Expectations, and Self-Selection Bias." *Contemporary Accounting Research* (Fall 1990): 142–172.

Accounting Standards Steering Committee. *The Corporate Report.* London: Accounting Standards Steering Committee, 1975.

Albrecht, W. D., and F. M. Richardson. "Income Smoothing by Economy Sector." *Journal of Business Finance and Accounting* (Winter 1990): 713–730.

American Accounting Association, "Committee on Accounting and Auditing Measurement, 1989–1990." *Accounting Horizons* (September 1991): 81–105.

Bannister, J. W., and A. Riahi-Belkaoui. "Value Added and Corporate Control in the U.S." *Journal of International Financial Management and Accounting* (Autumn 1991): 241–257.

Barlev, B., and H. Levy, "On the Variability of Accounting Numbers." *Journal of Accounting Research* (Autumn 1979): 305–315.

Barrett, M. J., W. H. Beaver, W. W. Cooper, J. A. Milburn, D. Solomons, and D. P. Tweedie. "Report of the American Accounting Association Committee on Accounting and Auditing Measurement, 1989–90." *Accounting Horizons* (September 1991): 81–105.

Beaver, W. H. "The Time Series Behavior of Earnings." *Empirical Research in Accounting: Selected Studies,* Supplement to *The Journal of Accounting Research* 8 (1970): 101–116.

Beaver, W., A. Christie, and P. Griffin. "The Informational Content of SEC Accounting Series Release 190." *Journal of Accounting Economics* (August 1990): 127–157.

Beaver, W., and R. Dukes. "Interperiod Tax Allocation, Earnings Expectations, and the Behavior of Security Prices." *Accounting Review* (April 1972): 320–322.

Beaver, W., P. A. Griffin, and W. R. Landsman. "The Incremental Information Content of Replacement Cost Earnings." *Journal of Accounting and Economics* 4 (1982): 15–39.

Beaver, W., R. Lambert, and D. Morse. "The Informational Content of Security Prices." *Journal of Accounting and Economics* (March 1980): 3–28.

———. "The Information Content of Security Prices: A Second Look." *Journal of Accounting and Economics* (July 1987): 139–157.

Beaver, W., and W. Landsman. *The Incremental Information Content of the FAS 33 Disclosures.* Stamford, CT: Financial Accounting Standards Board, 1983.

Beaver, W., and D. Morse. "What Determines Price-Earnings Ratio?" *Financial Analysts Journal* (July–August 1978): 65–76.

Belsley, D. A., E. Kuh, and R. E. Welsh. *Regression Diagnostics: Identifying Influential Data and Sources of Collinearity.* New York: Wiley, 1980.

Beneish, M. D., and C. R. Harvey. "The Specification of the Earnings-Returns Relation." Working Paper, Duke University, August 1993.

Bernard, V., and T. Sober. "The Nature and Amount of Information in Cash Flows and Accruals." *Accounting Review* (October 1989): 624–652.

Bernard, W., and R. Ruland. "The Incremental Information Content of Historical Cost and Current Cost Income Numbers: Time-Series Analyses for 1962–1980." *Accounting Review* (October 1987): 707–722.

Biddle, G., and F. Lindhal. "Stock Price Reactions to LIFO Adoptions: The Association between Excess Returns and LIFO Tax Savings." *Journal of Accounting Research* (Autumn 1982): 551–588.

Bildersee, J. S., J. J. Cheh, and C. Lee. "The International Price-Earnings Ratio Phenomenon." *Japan and the World Economy: International Journal of Theory and Policy* 2, no. 3 (1990): 263–282.

Black, F. "The Magic in Earnings: Economic Earnings Versus Accounting Earnings." *Financial Analysts Journal* (November–December 1980): 19–29.

Bublitz, B., T. J. Frecka, and J. C. McKeown. "Market Association Tests and FASB Statement No. 33 Disclosures: A Reexamination." *Journal of Accounting Research* (Supplement 1985): 1–23.

Cawing, C. S. A., W. S. Hopwood, and J. C. McKeown. "Nonlinearity and Specification Problems in Unexpected Earnings Response Regression Model." *The Accounting Review* (July 1992): 579–598.

Chambers, A. E., and S. H. Penman. "Timeliness of Reporting and the Stock Price Reaction to Earnings Announcements." *Journal of Accounting Research* 22 (1984): 21–47.

Choi, F. D. S., and G. G. Mueller. *International Accounting.* Englewood Cliffs, NJ: Prentice-Hall, 1992.

Collins, D., and S. Kothari. "A Theoretical and Empirical Analysis of the Determinants of the Relation between Earnings Innovations and Security Returns." *Journal of Accounting and Economics* (July 1989): 143–81.

Cox, B. *Value Added: An Appreciation for the Accounts Concerned with Industry.* London: Heinemann, 1978.

Deegan, C., and A. Hallam. "The Voluntary Presentation of Value Added Statements in Australia: A Political Cost Perspective." *Accounting and Finance* (May 1991): 1–29.

Drucker, P. F. "Reckoning with the Pension Fund Revolution." *Harvard Business Review* (March–April 1991): 106–114.

Easman, W., A. Falkenstein, and R. Weil. "The Correlation between Sustainable Income and Stock Returns." *Financial Analysts Journal* (September–October 1979): 44–48.

Easton, P. D., and T. S. Harris. "Earnings as an Explanatory Variable for Returns." *Journal of Accounting Research* (Spring 1991): 19–36.

Easton, P. D., and M. Zmijewski. "Cross-Sectional Variation in the Stock Market Response to Accounting Earnings Announcements." *Journal of Accounting and Economics* (July 1989): 117–141.

Fama, E. F., and M. H. Iller. *The Theory of Finance.* New York: Holt, Rinehard and Winston, 1972.

Financial Accounting Standards Board. *Statement of Financial Accounting Concepts No. 1: Objectives of Financial Reporting to Business Enterprises.* Stamford, CT: FASB, 1987.

Foster, T., D. Jenkins, and D. Vickrey. "Additional Evidence on the Incremental Content of the 10-k." *Journal of Business Finance and Accounting* (Spring 1983): 56–66.

Foster, T., and D. Vickrey. "The Incremental Information Content of the 10-k." *The Accounting Review* (October 1978): 921–934.

Freeman, R., J. Ohlson, and S. Penman. "Book Rate-of-Return and Prediction of Earnings Change: An Empirical Investigation." *Journal of Accounting Research* (Autumn 1982): 639–653.

Freeman, R. N., and S. Y. Tse. "A Nonlinear Model of Security Price Responses to Unexpected Earnings." *Journal of Accounting Research* (Fall 1992): 157–185.

Gray, S. J., and K. T. Maunders. *Value Added Reporting: Uses and Measurement.* London: Association of Certified Accountants, 1980.

Harmon, W. "Earnings vs. Fund Flows: An Empirical Investigation of Market Reaction." *Journal of Accounting, Auditing and Finance* (Fall 1984): 24–34.

Harris, G. J. "Value Added Statements." *The Australian Accountant* (May 1982): 261–264.

Hopwood, W., and T. Schaefer. "Incremental Information Content of Earnings and Nonearnings Based on Financial Ratios." *Contemporary Accounting Research* (Fall 1988): 318–342.

Hoskins, R. E., J. S. Hughes, and W. E. Ricks. "Evidence on the Incremental Information Content of Additional Firm Disclosures Made Concurrently with Earnings." In *Studies on Alternative Measures of Accounting Income,* Supplement to *The Journal of Accounting Research* (1986): 1–36.

Hughes, J. S., and W. E. Ricks. "Association between Forecast Errors and Excess Returns Near to Earnings Announcements." *The Accounting Review* 62 (1987): 158–175.

Imhoff, E. A., Jr. "Income Smoothing: A Case of Doubt." *Accounting Journal* (Spring 1977): 85–100.

Karpik, P., and A. Belkaoui. "The Relative Relationship Between Systematic Risk and Value Added Variables." *Journal of International Financial Management and Accounting* (Spring 1990): 259–276.

Kormendi, R., and R. Lipe. "Earnings Innovation, Earnings Persistence, and Stock Returns." *Journal of Business* (July 1987): 37–64.

Lang, M. "Time Varying Stock Price Responses to Earnings Induced by Uncertainty about the Time-Series Properties of Earnings." *Journal of Accounting Research* (Fall 1991): 229–260.

Lang, M., and M. McNichols. "Earnings Quality, Financial Distress and the

Incremental Information Content of Cash Flows." Working Papers, Stanford University, July 1990.

Lee, T., J. Livnat, and P. Zarowin. "Cash Flows and Accruals: Differential Valuation Implications." Working Paper, New York University, March 1990.

Lev, B. "On the Usefulness of Earnings Research: Lessons and Direction for Two Decades of Empirical Research." *Journal of Accounting Research: Current Studies on the Information Content of Accounting Earnings* (Supplement 1989): 153–192.

Lev, B., and J. A. Ohlson. "Market Based Empirical Research: A Review, Interpretation and Extensions." *The Journal of Accounting Research* (Supplement 1982): 239–322.

Lipe, R. C. "The Information Contained in the Components of Earnings." *Journal of Accounting Research,* (Supplement 1986): 37–68.

Livnat, J., and P. Zarowin. "The Incremental Information Content of Cash-Flow Components." *Journal of Accounting and Economics* (May 1990): 25–46.

Maunders, K. T. "The Decision Relevance of Value Added Reports." In *Frontiers of International Accounting: An Anthology,* edited by F. D. Choi and G. G. Mueller, 225–245. Ann Arbor, MI: UMI Research Press, 1985.

McLeary, S. "Value Added: A Comparative Study." *Accounting Organizations and Society* 8, no. 1 (1983): 31–56.

Meek, G. K., and S. J. Gray. "The Value Added Statement: Innovation for U.S. Companies?" *Accounting Horizons* (June 1988): 73–81.

Morley, M. F. "The Value Added Statement: A British Innovation." *The Chartered Accountant Magazine* (May 1978): 31–34.

———. "The Value Added Statement in Britain." The *Accounting Review* (May 1979): 618–689.

Rayburn, J. "The Association of Operating Cash Flow and Accrual with Security Returns." *Journal of Accounting Research* (Supplement 1986): 112–133.

Renshall, M., R. Allan, and K. Nicholson. *Added Value in External Financial Reporting.* London: Institute of Chartered Accountants in England and Wales, 1979.

Riahi-Belkaoui, A. *Valued Added Reporting: Lessons for the United States.* Westport, CT: Greenwood Press, 1992.

Rutherford, B. A. "Value Added as a Focus of Attention for Financial Reporting: Some Conceptual Problems." *Accounting and Business Research* (Summer 1977): 215–220.

Schaefer, T., and M. Kennelle. "Alternative Cash Flow Measures and Risk-Adjusted Returns." *Journal of Accounting, Auditing and Finance* (Fall 1986): 278–287.

Sinha, G. *Value Added Income.* Calcutta: Book World, 1983.

Stickells, S. C. "A Comparative Analysis of the Relationships of Price to Earnings and Price to Book Values." Master's thesis, MIT, May 1985.

Stober, T. "The Incremental Information Content of Financial Statement Disclosures: The Case of LIFO Inventory Liquidations." *Journal of Accounting Research* (Supplement 1986): 138–164.

Suojanen, W. W. "Accounting Today and the Large Corporation." *Accounting Review* (July 1954): 391–398.

White, H. "A Heteroskedasticity-Consistent Covariance Matrix Estimator and a Direct Test for Heteroskedasticity." *Econometrica* (May 1980): 817–838.

Wilson G. P. "The Relative Information Content of Accruals and Cash Flows: Combined Evidence at the Earnings Announcement and Annual Report Release Date." *Journal of Accounting Research* (Supplement 1986): 165–200.

———. "The Incremental Information Content of Accrual and Funds Components of Earnings after Controlling for Earnings." *Accounting Review* (April 1987): 293–322.

Chapter 4

Productivity, Profit, and Firm Value

INTRODUCTION

Financial statements can be viewed as providing both earnings and non-earnings information. The nonearnings information refers to all data items reported in annual financial statements other than earnings, including earnings components.[1] Various studies have shown the ability of nonearnings accounting variables to predict future earnings changes[2, 3] and information content.[4] The nonearnings variables examined were mostly descriptors that have been directly or indirectly tested in prior incremental information content studies under different approaches.[5] This chapter adds to this literature. More specifically, we focus on a nonearnings variable, productivity, and examine its role in the prediction of future profitability and firm valuation. Productivity is chosen as a target of investigation for the following reasons: (1) it has not been examined in previous research and (2) economists as well as accountants praise its importance in the efficient management of firms and valuation of firms.[6, 7, 8, 9]

This chapter relies on Ohlson's[10, 11] valuation model to explain how productivity affects firm value. Penman[12] and Bernard[13] relied on the same model to show that book value and future return on equity (ROE) are key components in the accounting valuation model. Using this framework, we first examine the impact of productivity on future ROE and then investigate whether productivity explains cross-sectional differences in market value incremental to those explained by book value and current ROE.

The results of this chapter indicate that productivity does not provide much information about future profitability incremental to that provided by current profit rate, but it does explain cross-sectional differences in market value incremental to that explained by book value and current profit rate.

BENEFITS OF PRODUCTIVITY

Productivity has been praised and researched by both economists and accounting researchers. First, economists maintain that productivity gains are the engine for economic growth and chief executive officers (CEOs) cite them as among the most important issues requiring their attention.[14, 15] Second, the new management accounting literature hypothesizes a positive association between a firm's value and its productivity, with the claim that a firm's value should eventually be increased by improving its productivity. Finally, studies on the national/macroeconomic level showed a relationship between market value of capital stock and productivity. On the firm level, it was shown that the association between firm value and productivity measures in the U.S. oil refining and apparel industries is higher than the association between firm value and earning measures in the Litzenberger and Rao valuation model.[16]

VALUE ADDED FOR THE MEASUREMENT OF PRODUCTIVITY

Value added is one possible measure of productivity that can be easily derived from published accounting numbers. It represents the total return of the firm earned by all providers of capital, plus employees and the government.

$$S - B = W + I + \text{DP} + \text{DD} + T + R \qquad (1)$$

$$S - B - \text{DP} = W + I + \text{DD} + T + R \qquad (2)$$

where

R = retained earnings,

S = sales revenue,

B = purchases of material and services,

W = wages,

I = interest,

DD = dividends,

T = taxes, and

DP = depreciation.

Equation (1) expresses the gross value added; equation (2) expresses the net value added. In both equations, the left side (the subtractive side) shows the value added (gross or net), and the right side (the additive side) shows the disposal value among the stakeholders.

The net value added is used in this chapter as a measure of wealth. When divided by either total assets or sales it provides this study's measures of productivity.

TEST MODELS

Productivity and the Prediction of Future Profitability

We use current ROE as a benchmark explanatory variable in the prediction of future profitability and add productivity as an additional variable.

$$\text{Model 1:} \quad \text{ROE}_{it+1} + B_0 + B_1\text{ROE}_{it} + e_{it}$$

where

$$\text{ROE}_{it+1} = \frac{X_{t+1}}{BV_{r0}},$$

X_{t+1} = net income for year $t + 1$, and

BV_{r0} = book value of common equity at the end of year t.

Model 1 is used as a first step to examine the role of current ROE in predicting future ROE. The second step is to incorporate productivity in the model and evaluate the incremental information it provides.

$$\text{Model 2:} \quad \text{ROE}_{it+1} = B_0 + B_1\text{ROE}_{it} + B_2\frac{\text{NVA}}{\text{TA}_{it}} + e_{it}$$

where

$$\frac{\text{NVA}}{\text{TA}} = \text{productivity measure,}$$

NVA = net value added, and

TA = total assets.

Total assets is used as a proxy for the size of the firm's operations.

Productivity and the Value of the Firm

A model can be used to explain cross-sectional differences in market value on the basis of accounting numbers.

A valuation equation is used to develop test models that examine the valuation implications of productivity within an accounting framework.

$$MV_t = BV_t + \sum_{\tau=1}^{\infty} \rho - \tau E_t(X_{t+\tau}^a) \tag{3}$$

where

MV_t = market value of the firm at the end of year t,

BV_t = book value of the firm at the end of year t,

ρ = one plus risk-free rate,

X_t^a = abnormal earnings = $X_t - (\rho - 1)BV_{t-1}$, and

X_t = accounting earnings.

Assuming that abnormal earnings follow an AR(1) process, we can rewrite equation (3) as follows.

$$MV_t = BV_t + \psi E_t(X_{t+1}^a) \tag{4}$$

where

$$\psi = \sum_{\tau=1}^{\infty} \rho^{-\tau}\phi^{\tau-1}$$

$$\phi = AR(1) \text{ parameter}$$

By replacing X_{t+1}^a with $X_{t+1} - (\rho - 1)BV_t$, we get

$$MV_t = BV_t + \psi E_t[X_{t+1} - (\rho - 1)BV_t] \tag{5}$$

Since $ROE_{t+1} = \dfrac{X_{t+1}}{BV_t}$, we can rewrite equation (5) in terms of ROE:

$$MV_t = \psi\left[1 - \rho + \frac{1}{\psi} + E_t(ROE_{t+1})\right]BV_t \tag{6}$$

By substituting $E_t(ROE_{t+1})$ with current accounting variables, as proposed by model 2 described in the previous section, we can express market value as a function of current accounting variables:

$$MV_t = \psi\left(1 - \rho + \frac{1}{\psi} + \beta_0 + \beta_1 ROE_t + \beta_2\frac{NVA_t}{TA}\right)BV_t \tag{7}$$

From equation (5), we develop the following test models:

Model 3: $MV_{it} = \gamma_0 + \gamma_1 BV_{it} + e_{it}$ (8)

Model 4: $MV_{it} = \gamma_0 + (\gamma_1 + \gamma_2 ROE_{it})BV_{it} + e_{it}$ (9)

Model 5: $MV_{it} = \gamma_0$

$$+ \left(\gamma_1 + \gamma_2 ROE_{it} + \gamma_3\frac{NVA_{it}}{TA}\right)BV_{it}$$

$$+ e_{it} \tag{10}$$

where

MV_{it} = market value of common equity per share for firm i at the end of year t,

BV_{it} = book value of common equity per share for firm i at the end of year t, and

$\dfrac{NVA}{TA}$ = net value added/total assets for firm i during year t.

SAMPLE SELECTION AND DESCRIPTIVE STATISTICS

Sample Selection

The availability of data for each of the variables included in models 1 to 5 defined the sample used. More specifically, these measures are defined from Compustat data items as follows:

Net value added (NVA) = the sum of labor expenses, corporate taxes, dividends, interest expense, minority shareholders in subsidiaries, and retained earnings;

BV_{it} = book value of common equity per share for firm i at the end of year t; and

MV_{it} = market value of common equity per share for firm i at the end of year t.

The firms examined in this study represent all the NYSE and AMEX firms that have available data over the period 1973–1990 in Compustat. The selection procedure resulted in a sample of 3,998 firm-year observations.

Descriptive Statistics and Correlation Analysis

Exhibits 4.1 and 4.2 present, respectively, the descriptive statistics and correlation analysis. Two noticeable results are the significant positive correlation between current and future profitability and the significant negative relationship between the book value of equity and the productivity measure.

Exhibit 4.1
Descriptive Statistics: 1973–1990

Variables	Mean	Standard Deviation	Median
ROE_t	0.0504	13.554	0.2522
ROE_{t+1}	0.0622	13.500	0.2459
NVA/TA	0.4823	0.289	0.4577
Total Assets	$4,205.87	9,642.71	1,128.27
Book Value of Equity	$1,544.82	3,484.77	453.65
Market Value of Equity	$2,382.42	5,268.42	632.97

Exhibit 4.2
Pearson and Spearman Correlation Coefficients: 1973–1990

	ROE_t	ROE_{it+1}	$(NVA/TA)_t$	Book Value of Equity
ROE_{it}	1.000	0.1813·	0.01061	0.00910
ROE_{it+1}		1.000	0.01394	0.00982
$(NVA/TA)_t$			1.000	-0.16714·
Book Value of Equity				1.000

*Significant at 99%

TEST RESULTS

Results on Future Profitability

Exhibit 4.3 shows the results on productivity and profitability. As reported for other studies, panel A shows that current ROE provides information about future ROE in all the years examined. However, with the exception of the results for 1989, panel B shows that productivity, as measured by net value added over total assets, does not provide information about a firm's profitability that is incremental to that provided by current profitability.

Exhibit 4.3
Productivity and Profitability

Panel A:
Model 1: $ROE_{it+1} = B_0 + B_1 ROE_{it} + e_{it}$

Year	Number of Firms	$B_0^{(i)}$	B_1	R^2 Adjusted
1973	173	0.1248 (6.405)*	0.5694 (8.529)*	29.31%
1974	169	0.0523 (2.453)*	0.6147 (8.843)*	31.36
1975	175	0.1374 (10.781)*	0.5880 (12.041)*	45.14
1976	187	0.0385 (2.476)**	0.8573 (16.412)*	58.93
1977	181	0.0948 (6.588)*	0.6981 (14.485)*	53.57
1978	182	0.0624 (3.112)*	0.7975 (12.227)*	44.93
1979	181	-0.0211 (-0.951)	0.8724 (12.425)*	45.87
1980	176	0.0242 (1.473)	0.7850 (13.553)*	50.94
1981	178	-0.0560 (-2.660)*	0.9000 (11.530)*	42.57
1982	183	0.0624 (3.112)*	0.6744 (8.413)*	27.60
1983	173	0.0726 (5.421)*	0.7285 (14.163)*	53.57
1984	179	-0.0808 (-2.858)*	1.1339 (10.973)*	40.02
1985	174	-0.1952 (-0.515)	-0.0009 (-0.004)	-0.58
1986	158	0.0796 (0.777)	0.1820 (9.280)*	35.01
1987	160	0.1714 (6.454)*	0.1111 (6.644)*	21.24
1988	199	-0.0128 (-0.225)	0.7509 (5.004)*	10.78
1989	194	0.0432 (1.494)	0.2331 (3.558)*	5.67
1990	205	-0.0629 (-1.785)***	0.8727 (9.228)*	29.10

Exhibit 4.3 (Continued)

Panel B:

Model 2: $ROE_{it+1} = B_0 + B_1 ROE_{it} + B_2 \frac{NVA}{TA}_{it} + e_{it}$

Year	Number of Firms	$B_0^{(i)}$	B_1	B_2	R^2 Adjusted
1973	173	0.1222 (4.821)*	0.5654 (7.903)*	0.0072 (0.160)	28.91%
1974	169	0.0569 (2.260)**	0.6213 (8.598)*	-0.0125 (-0.346)	31.00
1975	175	0.1208 (7.446)*	0.5704 (11.460)*	0.0421 (1.641)	45.67
1976	187	0.0294 (1.550)	0.8495 (15.996)*	0.0218 (0.835)	58.87
1977	181	0.0869 (4.946)*	0.6878 (13.753)*	0.0203 (0.781)	53.47
1978	182	0.0822 (3.450)*	0.8232 (12.262)*	-0.0515 (-1.525)	45.33
1979	181	0.0153 (0.486)	0.8938 (12.567)*	-0.0781 (-1.626)	46.36
1980	176	0.0344 (1.426)	0.7901 (13.460)*	-0.0201 (0.575)	42.31
1981	178	-0.0661 (-2.119)**	0.8984 (11.472)*	0.0201 (0.441)	42.31
1982	183	0.0220 (0.675)	0.6545 (8.085)*	0.0907 (1.506)	28.11
1983	173	0.0583 (3.135)*	0.7102 (13.159)*	0.0397 (1.109)	53.63
1984	179	-0.0947 (-2.846)*	1.1108 (10.341)*	0.0400 (0.795)	39.89
1985	174	-0.8543 (-1.330)	-0.0367 (-0.149)	1.4750 (1.269)	-0.23
1986	158	0.0106 (0.062)	0.1812 (9.193)*	0.1561 (0.502)	34.70
1987	160	0.1373 (2.726)*	0.1104 (6.586)*	0.0818 (0.799)	21.06

Exhibit 4.3 (Continued)

1988	199	0.0432 (0.485)	0.7648 (5.061)*	-0.1625 (-0.823)	10.63
1989	194	-0.0159 (-0.389)	0.2182 (3.336)*	0.1730 (2.024)*	7.16
1990	205	-0.0807 (-1.621)	0.8671 (9.090)*	0.0531 (0.506)	28.84

(i) White's (1980) heteroskedasticity-consistent t statistics are within parentheses.
   *Significant at $\alpha = 0.01$.
  **Significant at $\alpha = 0.05$.
 ***Significant at $\alpha = 0.10$.

Results on Market Value

Exhibit 4.4 shows the results on productivity and firm value. As expected from other studies, panel A shows that book value is related to the market value of equity for all years examined. Panel B shows that current profitability provides information about market value that is incremental to that provided by the book value of equity. The R^2 increased for each of the years examined. Panel C shows the incremental explanatory power of productivity as evidenced by the increase in R^2 from model 4 to model 5 for the 19 years examined.

SUMMARY AND CONCLUSIONS

This chapter shows that productivity is useful in understanding the role of accounting variables in the prediction of firm valuation. Productivity was measured by net value added over assets or sales. Given these results, an important accounting policy question is whether firms should be required to disclose the underlying data needed to compute value added variables and productivity. The current disclosure system does not mandate the disclosure of some of the information needed to compute the value added and productivity measure. At present less than 10 percent of the firms listed on Compustat consistently disclose labor expenses, a key variable. The cost of reporting this data should be relatively immaterial given the availability of such information. In addition, the

Exhibit 4.4
Productivity and Market Value

Panel A:
Model 3: $MV_{it} = Y_0 + Y_1 BV_{it} + e_{it}$

Year	Number of Firms	Y_0 [i]	Y_1	R^2 Adjusted
1973	272	6.2590 (5.929)*	0.6722 (16.088)*	55.47%
1974	206	0.7846 (1.027)	0.8095 (24.877)*	75.00
1975	218	-1.5815 (-0.993)	1.2216 (22.755)*	70.33
1976	228	-9.5742 (-3.945)*	1.9563 (29.979)*	79.75
1977	230	-16.6842 (-6.145)*	2.2627 (51.400)*	91.99
1978	236	-6.0312 (-4.516)*	1.3441 (82.152)*	96.62
1979	237	0.9542 (1.157)	0.8752 (108.314)*	98.02
1980	224	5.0904 (6.145)*	0.7827 (90.712)*	97.35
1981	211	0.0553 (0.061)	0.9400 (50.287)*	92.30
1982	208	3.7392 (4.941)*	0.8667 (60.731)*	94.66
1983	202	9.2502 (9.631)*	0.7469 (15.046)*	52.73
1984	203	7.2912 (7.879)*	0.7741 (16.707)*	57.81
1985	205	31.9156 (16.780)*	-0.5353 (-11.588)*	39.40
1986	194	16.4990 (9.422)*	0.6925 (8.208)*	25.49
1987	203	18.9504 (8.830)*	0.5481 (5.606)*	13.04
1988	257	16.6107 (11.005)*	0.6111 (9.207)*	24.58
1989	256	20.7116 (12.116)*	0.5720 (8.169)*	21.43
1990	256	17.6894 (12.963)*	0.5005 (9.419)*	25.52

Exhibit 4.4 (Continued)

Panel B:

Model 4: $MV_{it} = Y_0 + (Y_1 + Y_2 ROE_{it}) BV_{it} + e_{it}$

Year	Number of Firms	$Y_0^{(i)}$	Y_1	Y_2	R^2 Adjusted
1973	207	6.2579 (6.156)*	1.0549 (10.465)*	-0.8153 (-4.143)*	58.71%
1974	206	0.8408 (1.095)	0.6916 (4.721)*	0.2295 (0.826)	74.96
1975	218	-2.3880 (-1.589)	2.2678 (11.514)*	-2.1064 (-5.495)*	73.85
1976	228	-9.0124 (-3.614)*	1.5755 (4.003)*	0.6708 (0.981)	79.74
1977	230	-15.4817 (-5.868)	1.6933 (4.851)*	0.9284 ((1.645)	92.05
1978	236	-4.5413 (-3.918)*	2.4068 (20.644)*	-2.2593 (9.177)*	97.50
1979	237	3.6405 (5.051)*	1.3968 (28.580)*	-1.3307 (-10.772)*	98.67
1980	224	6.7157 (6.360)*	0.9314 (15.133)*	-0.5119 (-2.440)**	97.41
1981	211	5.1377 (5.571)*	1.2652 (33.760)*	-1.3163 (-9.547)*	94.61
1982	208	2.8974 (3.250)*	0.7656 (12.966)*	0.3662 (1.764)***	94.71
1983	202	7.9887 (8.855)*	0.3966 (5.518)*	1.0204 (6.294)*	60.35
1984	203	6.9028 (8.168)*	0.4010 (5.636)*	0.8648 (6.516)*	64.99
1985	205	19.3356 (9.462)*	-0.8807 (-16.828)*	2.7797 (9.684)*	58.34
1986	194	15.3530 (8.530)*	0.4759 (3.759)*	0.7255 (2.331)**	27.16
1987	203	18.9955 (8.725)*	0.5679 (3.215)*	-0.0542 (-0.135)	12.61
1988	257	16.6711 (11.137)*	0.4351 (4.331)*	0.5066 (2.318)**	25.85
1989	256	20.9558 (12.234)*	0.4082 (3.162)*	0.4480 (1.509)	20.83
1990	256	17.5512 (12.942)*	0.3449 (3.884)*	0.5246 (2.177)**	26.60

Exhibit 4.4 (Continued)

Panel C:

Model 5: $MV_{it} = V_0 + (V_1 + V_2 ROE_{it} + V_3 \frac{NVA}{TA}_{it}) BV_{it} + e_{it}$

Year	No. of Firms	$V^{(i)}_0$	V_1	V_2	V_3	R^2 Adj.
1973	207	5.7520 (5.054)	1.1515 (8.204)*	0.2844 (0.989)	-1.053 (3.385)*	58.75%
1974	206	0.7378 (0.938)	0.5058 (3.294)*	0.8569 (3.319)*	0.0933 (0.340)	76.13
1975	218	-2.7735 (2.997)	0.5077 (3.317)*	5.3630 (18.841)	-0.7806 (-3.170)*	90.09
1976	228	2.9896 (5.667)*	0.4923 (6.115)*	1.9027 (73.235)	-0.1664 (-1.206)	99.18
1977	230	2.9998 (6.629)*	0.5477 (9.873)*	1.1327 (96.084)	-0.1891 (-2.140)**	99.81
1978	236	4.3691 (9.034)*	0.304 (4.403)*	0.9570 (38.769)	0.0697 (0.642)	99.66
1979	237	4.9105 (9.783)*	0.3843 (5.418)*	0.8789 (16.205)	-0.0543 (-0.469)	99.37
1980	224	3.7593 (3.424)*	1.0796 (17.329)	0.7871 (6.003)*	-0.8545 (-4.206)*	97.76
1981	211	7.2701 (7.713)*	0.8987 (12.090)	-0.3557 (5.589)	-0.6646 (-3.850)*	95.29
1982	208	4.8131 (4.528)*	0.5990 (7.653)*	-0.2783 (3.157)	0.5618 (2.644)*	94.94
1983	202	7.7345 (8.627)*	0.4111 (5.775)*	0.3572 (2.492)**	0.8671 (5.056)*	61.36
1984	203	7.3743 (8.899)*	0.3681 (5.296)*	0.5102 (3.742)*	0.5884 (3.967)*	67.12
1985	205	13.1514 (6.929)*	0.3903 (2.511)**	0.0595 (8.543)*	0.7306 (2.124)**	69.25

Exhibit 4.4 (Continued)

1986	194	15.1733 (8.243)*	0.5052 (3.546)*	-0.0525 (-0.486)	0.6925 (2.170)**	28.87
1987	203	12.9702 (11.701)	0.6836 (7.781)*	0.9169 (24.791)	-0.1719 (-0.861)	78.44
1988	257	16.7107 (11.135)	0.4332 (4.304)*	0.0063 (0.542)	0.5058 (2.312)**	26.64
1989	256	19.9074 (11.670)	0.3982 (3.149)*	0.2412 (3.416)*	0.4496 (1.546)	24.02
1990	256	17.4030 (13.200)	0.2107 (2.275)**	0.4388 (3.996)*	0.7614 (3.152)*	30.68

(^{i}) White's (1980) heteroskedasticity-consistent t statistics are within parentheses.
  *Significant at $\alpha = 0.01$.
 **Significant at $\alpha = 0.05$.
***Significant at $\alpha = 0.10$.

FASB's Statement of Financial Accounting Concepts No. 5 notes that supplementary financial statements can be useful for introducing and gaining experience with new kinds of information.[17] The American Accounting Association Committee on Accounting and Auditing Measurement has recommended that value added be considered for mandatory disclosure.[18] The end result will be the availability of productivity measures to users of accounting information.

NOTES

    1. Ou, Jane A., "The Information Content of Nonearnings Accounting Numbers as Earnings Prediction," *Journal of Accounting Research* (Spring 1990): 144–163.

    2. Ou, Jane A., and S. H. Penman, "Financial Statement Analysis and Prediction of Stock Returns," *Journal of Accounting and Economics* 11 (1989): 295–325.

    3. Ou, Jane A., and S. H. Penman, "Accounting Measurement, Price-Earnings Ratio, and the Information Content of Security Prices," *Journal of Accounting Research* (Supplement 1989): 111–144.

    4. Ou, Jane A., "The Information Content of Nonearnings Accounting Numbers as Earnings Predictions," op. cit.

    5. Ibid., 148.

    6. Kaplan, R. S., "Measuring Manufacturing Performance: A New Chal-

lenge for Managerial Accounting Research," *The Accounting Review* (October 1983): 685–705.

7. Bailey, M. E., "Productivity and the Services of Capital and Labor," *Brookings Papers on Economic Activity* (April 1981): 1–65.

8. Kaufman, R. T., and R. A. Jacoby, "The Stock Market and the Productivity Slowdown: International Evidence," *Review of Economics and Statistics* (February 1986): 18–23.

9. Bao, Ben-Hsien, and Da-Hsien Bao, "An Empirical Investigation of the Association between Productivity and Firm Value," *Journal of Business Finance and Accounting* (Winter 1989): 699–718.

10. Ohlson, J. A., "Earnings, Book Values, and Dividends in Security Valuation," Working Paper, Columbia University (February 1991).

11. Ohlson, J. A., "Accounting Earnings, Book Value, and Dividends: The Theory of the Clean Surplus Equation," Working Paper, Columbia University (1988).

12. Penman, S. H., "Return to Fundamentals," *Journal of Accounting, Auditing and Finance* (Fall 1992): 465–483.

13. Bernard, V. L., "Accounting-Based Valuation Models, Determinants of Market-to-Book Ratios, and Implications for Financial Statement Analysis," Working Paper, University of Michigan (June 1993).

14. Horngren, C. T., G. Foster, and S. Datar, *Cost Accounting: A Managerial Emphasis* (Englewood Cliffs, NJ: Prentice-Hall), 772.

15. Drucker, P., "The New Productivity Challenge," *Harvard Business Review* (November–December 1991): 69–79.

16. Litzenberger, R. H., and C. U. Rao, "Estimates of the Marginal Rate of Time Preference and Average Risk Aversion of Investors in Electric Utility Shares: 1960–1966," *Bell Journal of Economics and Management Sciences* (Spring 1971): 265–277.

17. Financial Accounting Standards Board, *Statement of Financial Accounting Concepts No 5: Recognition and Measurement in Financial Statements of Business Enterprises* (Stamford, CT: FASB, 1984).

18. American Accounting Association, "Committee on Accounting and Auditing Measurement, 1989–1990," *Accounting Horizons* (September 1991): 81–105.

REFERENCES

American Accounting Association. "Committee on Accounting and Auditing Measurement, 1989–1990." *Accounting Horizons* (September 1991): 81–105.

Bailey, M. E. "Productivity and the Services of Capital and Labor." *Brookings Papers on Economic Activity* (April 1981): 1–65.

Bao, Ben-Hsien, and Da-Hsien Bao. "An Empirical Investigation of the Association Between Productivity and Firm Value." *Journal of Business Finance and Accounting* (Winter 1989): 699–718.

Bernard, V. L. "Accounting-Based Valuation Models, Determinants of Market-to-Book Ratios, and Implications for Financial Statement Analysis." Working Paper, University of Michigan, June 1993.

Bernard, V. L., and J. Noel. "Do Inventory Disclosures Predict Sales and Earnings?" *Journal of Accounting, Auditing and Finance* (Spring 1991): 145–181.

Drucker, P. "The New Productivity Challenge," *Harvard Business Review* (November–December 1991): 69–79.

Financial Accounting Standards Board. *Statement of Financial Accounting Concepts No 5: Recognition and Measurement in Financial Statements of Business Enterprises.* (Stamford, CT: FASB, 1984).

Horngren, C. T., G. Foster, and S. Datar. *Cost Accounting, A Managerial Emphasis.* Englewood Cliffs, NJ: Prentice-Hall, 1994.

Johnson, M. F., and D. W. Lee. "Financing Constraints and the Role of Cash Flow from Operations in the Prediction of Future Profitability." *Journal of Accounting, Auditing and Finance* (Forthcoming).

Kaplan, R. S. "Measuring Manufacturing Performance: A New Challenge for Managerial Accounting Research." *The Accounting Review* (October 1983): 685–705.

Kaufman, R. T., and R. A. Jacoby. "The Stock Market and the Productivity Slowdown: International Evidence." *Review of Economics and Statistics* (February 1986): 18–23.

Litzenberger, R. H., and C. U. Rao. "Estimates of the Marginal Rate of Time Preference and Average Risk Aversion of Investors in Electric Utility Shares: 1960–1966." *Bell Journal of Economics and Management Science* (Spring 1971): 265–277.

Ohlson, J. A. "Accounting Earnings, Book Value, and Dividends: The Theory of the Clean Surplus Equation." Working Paper, Columbia University, 1988.

———. "Earnings, Book Values, and Dividends in Security Valuation." Working Paper, Columbia University, February 1991.

Ou, Jane A. "The Information Content of Nonearnings Accounting Numbers as Earnings Predictors." *Journal of Accounting Research* (Spring 1990): 144–163.

Ou, Jane A. and S. H. Penman. "Financial Statement Analysis and Prediction of Stock Returns." *Journal of Accounting and Economics* 11, (1989): 295–325.

———. "Accounting Measurement, Price-Earnings Ratio, and the Information Content of Security Prices." *Journal of Accounting Research* (Supplement 1989): 111–144.

————. "Financial Statement Analysis and the Evaluation of Market-to-Book Ratios." Working Paper, University of California at Berkeley, April 1993.

Penman, S. H. "Return to Fundamentals." *Journal of Accounting, Auditing and Finance* (Fall 1992): 465–483.

White, H. "A Heteroskedasticity-Consistent Covariance Matrix Estimator and a Direct Test for Heteroskedasticity." *Econometrica* (May 1980): 1425–1460.

Chapter 5

Performance Plan Adoption
and Performance

INTRODUCTION

Many firms rely on performance plans to provide incentive[1] and tax
benefits[2,3] and align principal-agent interests.[4] These plans are incentive
compensation plans that can take different forms. They are usually different combinations of short-term performance plans based on any of
several accounting and market variables. The awards can be in the form
of cash, stock and stock options, stock appreciation rights, performance
shares, or participative units.[5,6] The awards, as set by the board at the
beginning of a multiple-year period, are earned by executives following
the conformity of the firm's accounting performance to accounting-based
goals. Therefore executives will strive to achieve high accounting performance to receive the awards specified by the performance plans.

Prior research on performance plans has focused on the ex ante determinants of performance plan adoption,[7] the stock market reaction to
performance plan adoptions.[8,9] Other research attempted to disentangle
other factors that the market uses to assess the impact of various incentive plans on shareholder wealth. Venkateswar[10] provided evidence that,
beyond a point, incentive effects of some plans are offset by effects of
equity dilution, and shareholder wealth is reduced. In addition, Gaver[11]
refuted earlier findings that performance plan adoptions significantly increase shareholder wealth, and warned about the "annual meeting ef-

fect" first observed by Brickley.[12] There is, however, no evidence on the association between performance plan adoption and ex post profitability. This chapter fills the gap; it differs from previous research in two ways. First, it examines profit performance rather than market performance. Second, it makes a distinction between owner-controlled and manager-controlled firms following the adoption of performance plans. In line with Berle and Means' thesis[13] on the deterioration in managerial efficiency associated with the separation of ownership and control, we hypothesize that, following the adoption of performance plans, profit performance will increase in owner-controlled firms and decrease in manager-controlled firms. A longitudinal study of the performance of 70 firms for ten years surrounding the adoption of performance plans supports the hypotheses for owner-controlled firms.

THE IMPACT OF PERFORMANCE PLAN ADOPTION ON VALUE ADDED AND EARNINGS

Askren et al.[14] examined the impact of performance plan adoption on firm performance using accounting measures of return and productivity. Exhibit 5.1 shows the sample of firms used for the treatment group and the control group. Exhibit 5.2 shows the descriptive statistics for these firms. The results of the study are shown in Exhibits 5.3 and 5.4. The results indicate that treatment and control firms do not differ significantly on accounting return and productivity measures in the five years immediately preceding and the five years immediately following the adoption of an accounting-based performance plan. These results may be due to the failure to account for the contingent effects of moderator variables. One contingent variable of importance in this case is the type of ownership structure adopted by the firm. Accordingly, in what follows the chapter examines the contingent impact of ownership structure in the relationship between performance plan adoption and performance.

THE CONTINGENCY OF OWNERSHIP STRUCTURE

Background and Hypothesis

The thesis on the deterioration in managerial efficiency associated with the separation of ownership and control characterizing the modern corporation, and various theorists, have examined the effects of such conflicts of interests on firm performance, and the disciplinary forces that

Exhibit 5.1
Sample Companies

Treatment Firm	Year of Plan Adoption	Control Firm
Akzona	1971	Schering-Plough
Sun Co. Inc.	1972	Royal Dutch
Crown Zellerbach	1973	Mead Corp.
Vulcan Materials Co.	1973	Anchor Hocking Corp.
Bemis Co.	1974	Great Northern Nekoosa
Bendix Corp.	1974	AMC
Monsanto Co.	1974	Dow Chemical
Navistar International	1975	Boeing
Owens-Illinois Inc.	1975	Owens Corning Fiberglass
Unocal Corp.	1975	Conoco Inc.
Atlantic Richfield	1976	Cities Service Co.
Nabisco Inc.	1976	Carnation
Emerson Electric	1977	Raytheon
Hobart Corp.	1977	Ex-Cell-O
Nalco Chemical	1977	Schering-Plough
Rockwell Intl. Corp.	1977	General Dynamics
Hershey Foods Corp.	1978	Staley (A.E.)
Phillips Petroleum Co.	1978	Cities Service Co.
Cincinnati Milacron Inc.	1979	Bucyrus-Erie/Becor Western
Corning Inc.	1979	National Gypsum
Koppers Co.	1979	Ethyl Corp.
United Technologies	1979	Boeing
Allied Signal	1980	Halliburton Co.
Black and Decker Corp.	1980	Clark Equipment Co.
Celanese Corp.	1980	Hercules Inc.
Cummins Engine	1980	Clark Equipment Co.
General Mills Inc.	1980	Carnation Co.
Owens Corning Fiberglass	1980	Brockway
Staley Continental Inc.	1980	Hormel (Geo. A) & Co.
Texas Instruments Inc.	1980	Raytheon Co.
General Motors Corp.	1982	Ford Motor Co.
Merck & Co.	1982	Hercules
Rexnord Inc.	1982	Clark Equipment Co.
Textron Inc.	1982	Lockheed

Source: Askren, B. J., J. W. Bannister, and E. L. Pavlik, "The Impact of Performance Plan Adoption on Value Added and Earnings," *Managerial Finance* 20, no. 9 (1994): 33. Reprinted with permission.

reduce managers' private returns (e.g., shirking and consumption of perquisites), that is, the market for corporate control,[15] the managerial labor market,[16] incentive contracts,[17, 18, 19] and debt.[20] Accordingly, we make a distinction between managers' and stockholders' interests in examining the profit performance of firms following the adoption of performance

Exhibit 5.2
Descriptive Statistics for Treatment and Control Firms Pre- and Postadoption[1]

Variable[2]	Pre-Adoption			Post-Adoption			t(Z)-statistic Treatment Firm Pre vs. Post	t(Z)-statistic Control Firm Pre vs. Post
	Treatment	Control	t(Z)-statistic T vs. C	Treatment	Control	t(Z)-statistic T vs. C		
NVA	1507.3 (606.0)	1101.8 (543.9)	0.46 (0.36)	2570.4 (1070.0)	1869.3 (781.6)	0.54 (0.52)	0.77** (2.05)	1.00* (1.90)
IBED	163.8 (84.8)	96.2 (70.3)	1.07 (0.50)	337.2 (107.0)	289.0 (142.6)	0.30 (0.04)	1.23 (1.54)	1.89* (1.97)**
TA	2370.3 (1027.9)	1903.8 (962.5)	0.40 (0.82)	4645.9 (1692.8)	3253.2 (1637.2)	0.68 (0.44)	1.10** (2.08)	1.16** (2.17)
SAL	3982.2 (1602.9)	3226.8 (1683.1)	0.32 (0.01)	7269.8 (3029.2)	5524.9 (2607.0)	0.49 (0.30)	0.91** (2.18)	1.02** (2.15)

*Significant at the 0.10 level.

**Significant at the 0.05 level.

[1]Pre-adoption (post-adoption) data are means for the five years preceding (following) performance plan adoption. When fewer than five years of data are available, only those years are used to calculate the means. Amounts under the Treatment and Control columns are cross-sectional mean (median) values for the variables, amounts in the t (Z) statistic column are Student's t (Wilcoxon Z) statistics.

[2]NVA = net value added, IBED = income before extraordinary items and discontinued operations, TA = total assets, and SAL = net sales.

Source: Askren, B. J., J. W. Bannister, and E. L. Pavlik, "The Impact of Performance Plan Adoption on Value Added and Earnings," Managerial Finance 20, no. 9 (1994): 34. Reprinted with permission.

plans. We view the firm as an imperfect and unstable risk-sharing arrangement among managers, employees, and the shareholders that is in flux rather than in equilibrium.[21] This distinction is based on the premises found in the literature on managerial discretion; that is, although stockholders are wealth maximizers requiring a maximization of efficiency, managers have a tendency to maximize personal utility functions that have remuneration, power, security, and status as major factors, requiring a maximization of firm size and diversity.[22, 23, 24, 25] The impact of ownership structure on profit performance following the adoption of a performance plan is assumed to differ depending on whether the firm is owner controlled or manager controlled.

Owner Control and Performance Plan Adoption

Shareholders are generally assumed to be value maximizers who view managers' responsibility to be the maximization of efficiency. With concentrated ownership, stockholders are better able to coordinate action and demand information that will enable them to overcome any information asymmetries and influence management's decisions and responsibility toward value maximization and strategies that are in the stockholders' interest. Performance plans are generally used in the stockholders' interest. Performance plans are generally used in this context as a tool by owners to provide managerial incentives to help align the interests of managers and owners. Following the adoption of the performance plan, owners expect managers to improve firm profit performance by working harder, lengthening their decision horizons, and becoming less risk-averse in their investment decisions. Failure to comply with these contractual agreements may expose the managers to different and less favorable employment conditions. Therefore, for owner-controlled firms, the adoption of performance plans will lead to an improvement in performance.

H_1: The adoption of performance plans in owner-controlled firms is associated with an increase in performance.

Management Control and Performance Plan Adoption

Two competing hypotheses characterize the relationship between firm performance and management stockholdings; namely, the convergence-of-interest hypothesis and the entrenchment hypothesis (see, for example,

Exhibit 5.3A
ANCOVA Results for Accounting-Based Performance Measures I

Panel A: Productivity Measures based on Labor Expense[1]

MODEL		NVA/LAB	IBED/LAB	NVA3/LAB	IBED3/LAB
F-VALUE		1.81	0.97	1.03	2.42
Pr>F		0.1173	0.4416	0.4038	0.0400

		F-VALUE			
TIME		0.06	0.49	0.11	0.01
TYPE		0.98	0.39	1.01	1.09
TIME*TYPE		0.01**	0.28	0.00*	0.00***
CHGTA		6.55**	2.79*	3.40*	7.67*
CHGNP		1.43	0.88	0.62	3.31*

LS MEANS

TIME					
	Pre-Adoption	1.4520	0.0625	1.4531	0.8372
	Post-Adoption	1.5190	0.0669	1.5121	0.9423
	Pr. (Pre=Post)	0.4296	0.7095	0.4930	0.4953

TYPE					
	Treatment (T)	1.5310	0.0683	1.5260	0.9833
	Control (C)	1.4410	0.0611	1.4380	0.7962
	Pr. (T=C)	0.2566	0.5199	0.2864	0.2040

*Significant at the 0.10 level.
**Significant at the 0.05 level.
***Significant at the 0.01 level.

[1]NVA/LAB = net value added divided by labor expense.

IBED/LAB = income before extraordinary items and discontinued operations divided by labor expense.

NVA3/LAB = net value added with three year window divided by labor expense.

IBED3/LAB = income before extraordinary items and discontinued operations with three year window divided by labor expense.

Demsetz and Lehn[26]; Morck, Schleifer, and Vishny[27]; and Ravenscraft and Sherer[28]).

According to the convergence-of-interest hypothesis, market value and profitability increase with management ownership. The dispersion of shareholders' ownership enables managers holding little equity in the firm to forego value (wealth) maximization and use corporate assets to benefit themselves rather than the shareholders. Similarly, the costs of

Exhibit 5.3B
ANCOVA Results for Accounting-Based Performance Measures I

Panel B: Productivity Measures based on Number of Employees[2]

MODEL		NVA/EMP	IBED/EMP	NVA3/EMP	IBED3/EMP
F-VALUE		6.83	1.85	6.83	2.76
Pr>F		0.0001	0.1087	0.0001	0.0215
F-VALUE					
TIME		29.15***	5.57**	31.72***	8.98***
TYPE		0.00	0.04	0.00	0.12
TIME*TYPE		0.01**	0.05*	0.07	0.02*
CHGTA		4.17**	3.36*	2.35	3.13*
CHGNP		0.81	0.23	0.01	1.58
LS MEANS					
TIME					
	Pre-Adoption	22.3651	1.0228	21.8280	12.5681
	Post-Adoption	37.0562	1.6176	38.4642	24.6405
	Pr. (Pre=Post)	0.0001	0.0339	0.0001	0.0040
TYPE					
	Treatment (T)	29.8083	1.3435	30.2360	19.2374
	Control (C)	29.6130	1.2960	30.0561	17.9712
	Pr. (T=C)	0.9416	0.8615	0.9510	0.7580

*Significant at the 0.10 level.
**Significant at the 0.05 level.
***Significant at the 0.01 level.

[2]NVA/EMP = net value added divided by number of employees.

IBED/EMP = income before extraordinary items and discontinued operations divided by number of employees.

NVA3/EMP = net value added with three year window divided by number of employees.

IBED3/EMP = income before extraordinary items and discontinued operations with three year window divided by number of employees.

Source: Askren, B. J., J. W. Bannister, and E. L. Pavlik, "The Impact of Performance Plan Adoption on Value Added and Earnings," *Managerial Finance* 20, no. 9 (1994): 35. Reprinted with permission.

deviating from value maximization decline as the manager's stake in the firm increases, because managers are less likely to squander corporate wealth when they bear a larger share of the costs.

According to the entrenchment hypothesis market value and profitability do not increase with management ownership. Fama and Jensen[29]

Exhibit 5.4A
ANCOVA Results for Accounting-Based Performance Measures II

Panel A: Return Measures Based on Total Assets[1]

MODEL		NVA/TA	IBED/TA	NVA3/TA	IBED3/TA
F-VALUE		3.22	6.63	4.97	6.56
Pr>F		0.0093	0.0001	0.0004	0.0001
	F-VALUE				
TIME		0.93	0.00	1.38	0.93
TYPE		0.18	0.08	0.28	0.20
TIME*TYPE		0.01***	0.53***	0.00***	0.45***
CHGTA		14.87	32.27	23.16	28.55
CHGNP		0.12	0.26	0.02	2.67*
LS MEANS					
TIME					
	Pre-Adoption	0.5973	0.0188	0.5865	0.2882
	Post-Adoption	0.5653	0.0188	0.5589	0.2800
	Pr. (Pre=Post)	0.3994	0.9785	0.4576	0.7704
TYPE					
	Treatment (T)	0.5760	0.0192	0.5660	0.2906
	Control (C)	0.5866	0.0185	0.5794	0.2776
	Pr. (T=C)	0.7651	0.6739	0.7083	0.6270

*Significant at the 0.10 level.
**Significant at the 0.05 level.
***Significant at the 0.01 level.

[1]NVA/TA = net value added divided by total assets.

IBED/TA = income before extraordinary items and discontinued operatioins divided by total assets.

NVA3/TA = net value added with three year window divided by total assets.

IBED3/TA = income before extraordinary items and discontinued operations with three year window divided by total assets.

have pointed out the offsetting costs associated with higher management stockholdings. If managers have a small stockholding, they will work toward value maximization as a result of factors that include market discipline, for example, the managerial labor market, and the product market,[30] and the market for corporate control. If managers hold a large enough proportion of a firm's stock, to have the voting power to guarantee their jobs, however, they may opt for non-value-maximization behavior.

Exhibit 5.4B
ANCOVA Results for Accounting-Based Performance Measures II

Panel B: Return Measures Based on Net Sales^2

MODEL	NVA/SAL	IBED/SAL	NVA3/SAL	IBED3/SAL
F-VALUE	0.55	2.45	1.08	2.17
Pr>F	0.7381	0.0377	0.3772	0.0622

	F-VALUE			
TIME	0.80	0.08	1.55	0.89
TYPE	1.15	0.47	0.90	0.54
TIME*TYPE	0.00	0.26**	0.04*	0.22***
CHGTA	0.62	11.41	2.74	8.72
CHGNP	0.18	0.05	0.16	0.48

LS MEANS

TIME				
Pre-Adoption	0.3713	0.0123	0.3715	0.1942
Post-Adoption	0.3519	0.0120	0.3482	0.1791
Pr. (Pre=Post)	0.3451	0.8366	0.2452	0.5379

TYPE				
Treatment (T)	0.3718	0.0127	0.3694	0.1954
Control (C)	0.3513	0.0116	0.3503	0.1780
Pr. (T=C)	0.2816	0.4400	0.3223	0.4571

*Significant at the 0.10 level.
**Significant at the 0.05 level.
***Significant at the 0.01 level.

^{2}NVA/SAL = net value added divided by net sales.

IBED/SAL = income before extraordinary items and discontinued operations divided by net sales.

NVA3/SAL = net value added with three year window divided by net sales.

IBED3/SAL = income before extraordinary items and discontinued operations with three year window divided by net sales.

Source: Askren, B. J., J. W. Bannister, and E. L. Pavlik, "The Impact of Performance Plan Adoption on Value Added and Earnings," *Managerial Finance* 20, no. 9 (1994): 38. Reprinted with permission.

The two hypotheses, supported by Belkaoui and Pavlik[31] imply that performance will be positively related to lower ranges of management ownership and negatively to higher ranges of management ownership.

Performance awards can often lead to an increase in the range of management ownership in manager-controlled firms. From the lawsuits filed by shareholder groups, an argument can also be used against the notion that incentive plans in management controlled firms increase shareholder wealth.[32, 33] Similarly, Williamson[34] found some evidence that salary plus bonus was significantly higher for manager-controlled firms than for other types of firms, and viewed this finding as supportive of his theory that managers will use their discretion to pay themselves more. Under these circumstances, the discussion above implies that profitability in manager-controlled firms may either decrease or not change following performance plan adoption. The following research hypothesis is examined in the subsequent empirical study:

H_2: The adoption of performance plans in management-controlled firms is associated with a decrease in performance.

Methods

Sample and Methodology

A list of 130 firms voting on incentive plans for the period 1971–1982 period was obtained from previous research and through proxy examination. Information regarding incentive plan adoption was obtained from proxy statements filed with the Securities and Exchange Commission (SEC). Proxy statements containing contaminating information other than the proposed compensation plan, the election of directors, and the ratification of directors were excluded from the list. Proxy statements with missing SEC "stamp dates" were also excluded from the list. The procedure resulted in a usable sample of 70 firms. The list of firms and the year of adoption of the performance plan are shown in the Appendix.

A longitudinal design is used to capture the effects over time of the implementation of a performance plan. Data for two measures of performance were collected for year −5 through year +5 (relative to the year of adoption). In addition, one covariate (annual asset growth rate) and a control variable (industry membership) were used.

Performance Measures Used

The central performance measures used in this chapter were time series of profitability ratios over 11 years, including 5 years before and 5 years after the year of adoption. All series excluded the year of adoption to

Exhibit 5.5
Results of the Overall Analysis of Covariance for Operating Profit/Assets

Sources	F	P > F
1. Model	20.76	0.0001
2. Ownership Structure (A)	37.99	0.0001
3. Performance Plan Adoption (B)	7.16	0.0076
4. A x B	6.97	0.0085
5. Control Variables		
Industry	4.32	0.0379
6. Covariate		
Annual Asset Growth Rate	47.37	0.0001

avoid confounding the performance measures with related outcomes during the transition.[35] For purposes of analysis the profitability ratios were pooled by ownership structure types. The two profitability ratios used were (a) operating profit/total assets and (b) net profit/total assets. Operating profit over total assets was used to differentiate between profitability arising from the operations of the firm and total profitability.

Control Variable and Covariate

One control variable, industry, and one covariate, annual asset growth rate, were used to control for possible intervening effects.

With the length of time covered by the data, direct industry effects on performance or via type of ownership structure were possible. To control for direct industry effects, the SIC two-digit codes were used as a cat-

Exhibit 5.6
**Results of the Overall Analysis of Covariance for Net Profit/
Assets**

Sources	F	P > F
1. Model	18.94	0.0001
2. Ownership Structure (A)	40.64	0.0001
3. Performance Plan Adoption (B)	4.86	0.0279
4. A * B	5.47	0.0196
5. Control Variables		
Industry (SIC Codes)	5.79	0.0001
6. Covariate		
Annual Asset Growth Rate	37.96	0.0001

egorical control variable. All firms were captured through 12 industry codes.

Annual asset growth rate is included as a covariate motivated by the suggestion that firms may sacrifice profitability in periods of growth, and its use in studies of industrial structure as a proxy for industrial growth.

Ownership Structure

Various control criteria have been used in the literature. This chapter adopts the thesis that management control is achieved when ownership is diverse enough that it is difficult for a single owner to effectively control the selection of the board or form a coalition among owners.[36] Accordingly the following procedure was adopted:

1. From the proxy statement in the year of adoption of the performance plan the proportion of stock held by the five largest stockholders was determined.[37]

Exhibit 5.7
Tests and Variable Means and Standard Deviation by Ownership Structure Type before and after Performance Plan Adoption

Measures	Before Performance Plan Adoption	After Performance Plan Adoption	Pr > T
A. Owner Controlled Firms			
1. Operating Profit/Assets	0.3004	0.3748	0.0002*
2. Net Profit/Assets	0.2638	0.32509	0.0014*
B. Management Controlled			
Firms	0.4151	0.4115	0.8683
1. Operating Profit/Assets	0.3747	0.3692	0.7955
2. Net Profit/Assets			

*Significant at $\alpha = 0.01$.

2. For our sample, the median of the proportion of stock held by the five largest stockholders was 18.36 percent.

3. Firms where the five largest stockholders held a percentage higher than 18.36 percent were classified as owner controlled, whereas those with a percentage lower than 18.36 percent were classified as manager controlled.[38]

Data Analysis and Results

An overall analysis of covariance is used to test the overall relationship among (1) performance plan adoption and performance, (2) type of ownership structure and performance, and (3) the interactive effect of performance plan adoption and ownership structure on performance. Industry membership is a control variable. Annual asset growth is a covariate. An F test is used to test the difference between the dependent variable of profit performance measures after controlling for the control and covariate variables.

Exhibits 5.5 and 5.6 present the results of the analysis of covariance for operating profit over total assets and net profit over total assets for the firms in the sample. The results of the overall analysis of covariance are significant. The results suggest that the relationships between ownership structure and performance, between performance plan adoption and performance, and between ownership structure-performance plan adoption interactions and performance are statistically significant. The results show that the performance plan adoption has a differential effect on performance depending on ownership structure.

The impact of the adoption of a performance plan on profit performance is further investigated by performing mean comparisons before and after the adoption of performance plan by ownership structure. Exhibit 5.7 presents these results. The exhibit indicates that following the adoption of the performance plan (a) owner-controlled firms experienced a statistically significant increase in performance as hypothesized in H_1 and (b) manager-controlled firms experienced a decrease, although not statistically significant, in performance as hypothesized in H_2.[39]

Discussion

The central proposition of this chapter is that the adoption of a performance plan leads to different profitability changes in firms that have different ownership structures: owner controlled versus manager controlled. The results of this chapter support the contingency view of ownership structure in the relation between profitability and the adoption of performance plan.

Hypothesis 1 was supported, suggesting that the implementation of a performance plan in owner-controlled firms is associated with an increase in profitability. Hypothesis 2 was not supported.

The results verify the general contention that performance plans are an ideal tool for owners to provide managerial incentives to help align the interests of managers and owners. The adoption of performance plans by owner-controlled firms creates an incentive for managers to work harder, lengthen their decision horizons, and improve profit performance. The situation is different in manager-controlled firms where managers have guaranteed their jobs and used their discretion to improve their compensation and are not in any ''pressure'' situation for profitability improvement.

The adoption of a performance plan appears to be a more efficient mechanism for profitability enhancement in owner-controlled than in manager-controlled firms.

Another explanation for our results is the possibility that the performance plans adopted by manager-controlled firms have such easy goals that not much of an increase in performance followed adoption. In contrast, owner-controlled firms insist on challenging performance goals that lead to significantly higher profits. Firms are not obliged to report the performance goals for their plans and most of the firms in our sample did not, making it difficult to test the plausibility of this explanation.

Other limitations of the present chapter call for more research on the subject. First, although the results are insensitive to the current classification rule in the range of 15 to 20 percent, future research may have to examine the impact of different classification rules. Second, different measures of profitability and especially measures of productivity need to be used in the same context to verify the robustness of the thesis of this chapter. Third, the control and covariate variable in this chapter were limited to industry effect and annual asset growth rate. Other control and covariate variables need to be examined. Examples include early versus late adopters of performance plans and various risks measures. Fourth, future research needs to expand the analysis to control firms—nonadopters—to verify if the performance plan adoption or the ownership structure is driving the results. Fifth, a differentiation between firms where adoption is expected to influence short-term profitability and firms focusing on long-term profitability is warranted in future research. Finally, the current classification rule implicitly ensures that half the sample of performance plan adopters is manager controlled and the other half is owner controlled. Ignoring the effects of managerial entrenchment, agency costs related to the divergence of interests between owners and managers are inversely related to the degree of managerial ownership. Thus, manager-controlled firms face larger agency costs than owner-controlled firms. Manager-controlled firms will therefore seek to reduce the costs by adopting incentive arrangements such as performance plans. This suggests that future research should recognize that the incidence of performance plan adoptions will be higher in manager-controlled than in owner-controlled firms.

NOTES

1. Smith, C. W., and R. L. Watts, "Incentive and Tax Effects of U.S. Executive Compensation Plans," *Australian Journal of Management* 7 (1982): 39–157.

2. Miller, M. H., and M. S. Scholes, "Executive Compensation, Taxes and Incentives," in *Financial Economics: Essays in Honor of Paul Cootner,* ed. K. Cootner, and W. Sharpe, (Englewood Cliffs, NJ: Prentice-Hall, 1981): 55–63.

3. Hite, G. L., and M. S. Long, "Tax and Executive Stock Options," *Journal of Accounting and Economics* 4 (1982): 3–14.

4. Jensen, M., and W. Meckling, "Theory of the Firm: Managerial Behaviour, Agency Costs and Ownership Structure," *Journal of Financial Economics* 3 (1976): 305–360.

5. Kaplan, R., *Advanced Management Accounting* (Englewood Cliffs, NJ: Prentice-Hall, 1982).

6. Gaver, J. J., and K. M. Gaver, "The Association Between Performance Plan Adoption and Corporate Capital Investment: A Note," *Journal of Management Accounting Research* (Fall 1993): 145–158.

7. Gaver, J. J., "Incentive Effects and Managerial Compensation Contracts: A Study of Performance Plan Adoption," *Journal of Accounting, Auditing, and Finance* (Spring 1992): 137–156.

8. Larcker, D. F., "The Association between Performance Plan Adoption and Corporate Capital Investment," *Journal of Accounting and Economics* 5 (1983): 9–30.

9. Tehranian, H., and J. F. Waegelein, "Market Reaction to Short-Term Executive Compensation Plan Adoption," *Journal of Accounting and Economics* 7 (1985): 131–144.

10. Venkateswar, S., "Market Reaction to Long-Term Incentive Plan Adoption: Equity Dilution as an Explanatory Variable," *British Accounting Review* 24 (1992): 67–76.

11. Gaver, J. J., "Incentive Effects and Managerial Compensation Contracts: A Study of Performance Plan Adoptions," *Journal of Accounting, Auditing and Finance* (Spring 1992): 137–156.

12. Brickley, J. A., "Interpreting Common Stock Returns Around Proxy Statement Disclosures and Annual Shareholder Meetings," *Journal of Financial and Quantitative Analysis* 21 (1986): 343–349.

13. Berle, A. A., and G. C. Means, *The Modern Corporation* (New York: Macmillan, 1932).

14. Askren, Barbara J., James W. Bannister, and Ellen Pavlik, "The Impact of Performance Plan Adoption on Value Added and Earnings," *Managerial Finance* 20, no. 9 (1994): 27–43.

15. Manne, H. G., "Mergers and the Market for Corporate Control," *Journal of Political Economy* 73 (1965): 110–120.

16. Fama, E. F., "Agency Problems and the Theory of the Firm," *Journal of Political Economy* 88 (1980): 288–307.

17. Shavell, S., "Risk Sharing and Incentives in the Principal and Agent Relationship," *Bell Journal of Economics* 10 (1979): 55–73.

18. Holstrom, B., "Moral Hazard and Observability," *Bell Journal of Economics* 13 (1982): 324–340.

19. Holstrom, B., "Moral Hazard and Observability," *Bell Journal of Economics* 10 (1979): 74–91.

20. Jensen, M., "Agency Costs of Free Cash Flow, Corporate Finance, and Takeover," *The American Economic Review* 26 (1986): 323–399.

21. Coffee, J. A., "Shareholders Versus Managers: The Strain in Corporate Web," in *Knights, Raiders, and Targets: The Impact of the Hostile Takeover,* ed. J. C. Coffee (Oxford: Oxford University Press, 1988): 65–78.

22. Hunt, H. G. III, "The Separation of Corporate Ownership and Control: Theory, Evidence and Implications," *Journal of Accounting Literature* 5 (1986): 85–124.

23. Galbraith, J. K., *The New Industrial State* (New York: New American Library, 1967).

24. Marris, R., *The Economic Theory of Managerial Capitalism* (London: Macmillan, 1964).

25. Williamson, O. E., *The Economics of Discretionary Behavior: Managerial Objectives in a Theory of the Firm* (Englewood Cliffs, NJ: Prentice-Hall, 1964).

26. Demsetz, H., and K. Lehn, "The Structure of Corporate Ownership: Theory and Consequences," *Journal of Political Economy* 93 (1985): 1155–1177.

27. Morck, R. A., A. Schleifer, and R. W. Vishny, "Management Ownership and Market Valuation: An Empirical Analysis," *Journal of Financial Economics* 20 (1988): 293–315.

28. Ravenscraft, D., and F. M. Shere, "Life after Takeover," *The Journal of Industrial Economics* 36 (1987): 147–156.

29. Fama, E. F., and M. C. Jensen, "Agency Problems and Residual Claims," *Journal of Law and Economics* 20 (1983): 327–349.

30. Hart, O. D., "The Market Mechanism as an Incentive Scheme," *Bell Journal of Economics* 14 (1983): 366–382.

31. Belkaoui, A., and E. Pavlik, "The Effects of Ownership Structure and Diversification Strategy on Performance," *Managerial and Decision Economics* 13 (1992): 343–352.

32. Jones, T. M., "An Empirical Examination of the Resolution of Shareholder Derivative and Class Action Lawsuits," *Boston University Law Review* 22 (1980): 5–19.

33. Jones, T. M., "What's Bothering Those Shareholder-Plaintiffs?" *California Management Review* 22 (1980): 5–19.

34. Williamson, O. E., *The Economics of Discretionary Behavior: Managerial Objectives in a Theory of the Firm* (Englewood Cliffs, NJ: Prentice-Hall, 1964).

35. The results of this chapter did not change with the exclusion of the year before and after adoption.

36. Larner, R. J., *Management Control and the Large Corporation* (New York: Dunellen Publishing Company, 1970).

37. In our sample the five largest shareholders were all outside owners.

38. The empirical results observed in this study held with the classification rule fluctuating from 15 to 20%.

39. Similar results were obtained on testing the pairwise differences in medians.

REFERENCES

Aoki, M. *The Co-Operative Game Theory of the Firm.* Oxford: Clarendon Press, 1984.

Askren, B. J., James W. Bannister, and Ellen Pavlik. "The Impact of Performance Plan Adoption on Value Added and Earnings." *Managerial Finance* 20, no. 9 (1994): 27–43.

Belkaoui, A., and E. Pavlik. "The Effects of Ownership Structure and Diversification Strategy on Performance." *Managerial and Decision Economics* 13 (1992): 343–352.

Berle, A. A., and G. C. Means. *The Modern Corporation.* New York: Macmillan, 1932.

Brickley, J. A. "Interpreting Common Stock Returns Around Proxy Statement Disclosures and Annual Shareholder Meetings." *Journal of Financial and Quantitative Analysis* 21, (1986): 343–349.

Brickley, J. A., S. Bhagat, and R. C. Lease. "The Impact of Long-Range Managerial Compensation Plans on Shareholder Wealth." *Journal of Accounting and Economics* 7 (1985): 115–129.

Coffee, J. A. "Shareholders Versus Managers: The Strain in Corporate Web." In *Knights, Raiders, and Targets: The Impact of the Hostile Takeover,* edited by J. C. Coffee, 65–78. Oxford: Oxford University Press, 1988.

Demsetz, H. "The Structure of Ownership and the Theory of the Firm." *Journal of Law and Economics* 26 (1983): 357–390.

Demsetz, H., and K. Lehn. "The Structure of Corporate Ownership: Theory and Consequences." *Journal of Political Economy* 93 (1985): 1155–1177.

Fama, E. F. "Agency Problems and the Theory of the Firm." *Journal of Political Economy* 88 (1980): 288–307.

Fama, E. F., and M. C. Jensen. "Agency Problems and Residual Claims." *Journal of Law and Economics* 20 (1983): 327–349.

Galbraith, J. K. *The New Industrial State.* New York: New American Library, 1967.

Gaver, J. J. "Incentive Effects and Managerial Compensation Contracts: A Study of Performance Plan Adoptions." *Journal of Accounting, Auditing and Finance* 20 (Spring 1992): 137–156.

Gaver, J. J., and K. M. Gaver. "The Association Between Performance Plan Adoption and Corporate Capital Investment: A Note." *Journal of Management Accounting Research* 5 (Fall 1993): 145–158.

Gaver, J. J., K. M. Gaver, and G. P. Battistel. "The Stock Market Reaction to Performance Plan Adoptions." *The Accounting Review* 67 (January 1992): 172–182.

Hart, O. D. "The Market Mechanism as an Incentive Scheme." *Bell Journal of Economics* 14 (1983): 366–382.

Hite, G. L., and M. S. Long. "Tax and Executive Stock Options." *Journal of Accounting and Economics* 4 (1982): 3–14.

Holmstrom, B. "Moral Hazard and Observability." *Bell Journal of Economics* 10 (1979). 74–91.

———. "Moral Hazard and Observability." *Bell Journal of Economics* 13 (1982): 324–340.

Hunt, H. G., III. "The Separation of Corporate Ownership and Control: Theory, Evidence and Implications." *Journal of Accounting Literature* 5 (1986): 85–124.

Jensen, M. "Agency Costs of Free Cash Flow, Corporate Finance, and Takeover." *The American Economic Review* 26 (1986): 323–399.

Jensen, M., and W. Meckling. "Theory of the Firm: Managerial Behaviour, Agency Costs and Ownership Structure." *Journal of Financial Economics* 3 (1976): 305–360.

Jensen, M., and R. Ruback. "The Market for Corporate Control: The Scientific Evidence." *Journal of Financial Economics* 11 (1983): 5–50.

Jones, T. M. "An Empirical Examination of the Resolution of Shareholder Derivative and Class Action Lawsuits." *Boston University Law Review* 22 (1980): 5–19.

———. "What's Bothering Those Shareholder-Plaintiffs?" *California Management Review* 22 (1980): 5–19.

Kaplan, R. *Advanced Management Accounting* Englewood Cliffs, NJ: Prentice-Hall, 1982.

Larcker, D. F. "The Association between Performance Plan Adoption and Corporate Capital Investment." *Journal of Accounting Economics* 5 (1983): 9–30.

Larner, R. J. *Management Control and the Large Corporation.* New York: Dunellen Publishing Company, 1970.

Manne, H. G. "Mergers and the Market for Corporate Control." *Journal of Political Economy* 73 (1965): 110–120.

Marris, R. *The Economic Theory of Managerial Capitalism.* London: Macmillan, 1964.

Miller, M. H., and M. S. Scholes. "Executive Compensation, Taxes and Incentives." In *Financial Economics: Essays in Honor of Paul Cootner*, edited by K. Cootner and W. Sharpe, 55–63. Englewood Cliffs, NJ: Prentice-Hall, 1981.

Morck, R. A., A. Schleifer, and R. W. Vishny. "Management Ownership and Market Valuation: An Empirical Analysis." *Journal of Financial Economics* 20 (1988): 293–315.

Ravenscraft, D., and F. M. Sherer. "Life After Takeover." *The Journal of Industrial Economics* 36 (1987): 147–156.

Scherer, F. M. *Industrial Market Structure and Economic Performance*. Chicago: Rand McNally & Co, 1980.

Shavell, S. "Risk Sharing and Incentives in the Principal and Agent Relationship." *Bell Journal of Economics* 10 (1979): 55–73.

Smith, C. W., and R. L. Watts. "Incentive and Tax Effects of U.S. Executive Compensation Plans." *Australian Journal of Management* 7 (1982): 39–157.

Tehranian, H., N. G. Travlos, and J. W. Waegelein. "Management Compensation Contracts and Merger-Induced Abnormal Returns." *Journal of Accounting Research* 25 (Supplement 1988): 51–84.

Tehranian, H., and J. F. Waegelein. "Market Reaction to Short-Term Executive Compensation Plan Adoption." *Journal of Accounting and Economics* 7 (1985): 131–144.

Venkateswar, S. "Market Reaction to Long-Term Incentive Plan Adoption: Equity Dilution as an Explanatory Variable." *British Accounting Review* 24 (1992): 67–76.

Williamson, O. E. *The Economics of Discretionary Behavior: Managerial Objectives in a Theory of the Firm*. Englewood Cliffs, NJ: Prentice-Hall, 1964.

APPENDIX: SAMPLE OF FIRMS

Name of Firm	Year of Adoption
Akzona	71
Allied Steel	80
AMF	80
Armstrong Rubber	82
Ashland Oil	79
Atlantic Richfield	76
Baxter Travenol	82
Beatrice Foods	78
Bemis	74
Bendix	74
Black & Decker	80
Bristol Meyers	78
Burroughs	82
Cabot	72
Celanese	80
Central Soya	81
Cincinnati Milacron	79
Combustion Eng.	78
Cooper Labs	78
Corning Inc.	79
Crown Zellerbach	73
Datapoint	79
Diamond Shamrock	80
Dover	74
Eaton	74
Emerson Elec.	77
Ferro	82
FMC	73
General Mills	80
General Motors	82
Hershey Foods	78

Hobart	77
Honeywell	78
Illinois Toolworks	80
International Harvester	75
Koppers	79
Manville	78
Merck	82
Minnesota Mining	81
Monsanto	74
Nabisco	76
NALCO	77
Nashua	81
NCR	82
NL Industries	78
Outboard Marine	82
Owens Corning	80
Owens Illinois	75
Phillips Petroleum	78
Pillsbury	75
Ralston Purina	75
Rexnord	82
Roblin	77
Rockwell	77
Sanders Associates	80
Sealed Power	78
Shell	79
Singer	81
Squibb	75
Staley Continental Inc.	80
Sun Co.	72
Sybron	81
Texas Instruments	80
Textron	82
Toro	76

Chapter 6

The Systematic Risk and Value Added Variables

INTRODUCTION

Value added, a measure of wealth created and attributable to all stake-holders, is advocated as an important European innovation worthy of inclusion in U.S. company annual reports. Being utilitarian in nature, the ultimate test of any accounting innovation is its usefulness. One test of utility is the connection of the information to its function in capital markets. This is the spirit of early works establishing the empirical/theoretical relationship between accounting variables and market risk.[1] Accordingly, the main objective of this chapter is to test the incremental abilities of value added measures to explain cross-sectional variations in market betas beyond that provided by earning-based and cash flow–based risk measures.

RATIONALE

Various advantages are claimed in favor of the value added report, with the suggestion that it may become an innovation for U.S. corpo-

Portions of Chapter 6 are adapted from: Karpik, P., and A. Belkaoui, "The Relative Relationship between Systematic Risk and Value Added Variables," *Journal of International Financial Management and Accounting,* 1, no. 3 (1990): 259–276. Reprinted with permission.

rations. These advantages include (a) its use to measure wealth created by the company, to emphasize stakeholder interdependence, to condition employees' expectations regarding pay and prospects, and for productivity incentive schemes;[2] (b) its potential benefit as a ratio component in financial analysis and prediction of important economic events of interest to the firm; (c) its measure of the size and importance of firms; and (d) its use to conduct collective bargaining.[3] Although all the preceding claims need to be submitted to some form of empirical investigation, the concern in this chapter is with the relative ability of value added concepts to explain market risk. Two arguments are used.

The first argument, suggested by Maunders,[4] is that value added reporting is potentially useful to employees in their collective bargaining with the firm. It would affect their aspirations and those of their negotiating representatives. Basically, the value added report can be used by labor as a measure of "relative equity," because it reveals the comparative shares of each of the stakeholder groups in the firm's net output for a given period and the firm's "ability to pay." Labor's demand for increases in their share of the value added follows changes in earnings and other distributions of value added. Value added appears to offer a useful tool for a prediction of earnings, the expected returns, and total risk associated with securities. As stated by Maunders:

Value added information can affect the conduct of collective bargaining and hence the company's future labor costs. Unless such changes in labor costs are exactly canceled by increases in the values of output (an unlikely coincidence), company earnings will also change. So, on the presumption that we are able to show . . . that value added information may affect collective bargaining, we can also deduce that it is potentially useful to investors for forecasting a company's earnings and, hence, the expected returns and total risk associated with securities.[5]

The second argument follows from the evidence that indicates a relationship between earnings measures and security prices. More specifically, the empirical evidence on the relationship between accounting-based measures and market-based measures, from the initial study of Beaver and Manegold[6] to the more conclusive studies of Rosenberg and Grey[7] and Rosenberg and Guy,[8] suggests that the information provided by some accounting measures is consistent with the underlying information set used by investors to asses the riskiness of securities. If the benefits of value added, outlined earlier in the chapter, indicate a better measure of the total return of the firm, the value added series will produce a risk measure that is a better proxy of market risk than the corresponding cash flow and/or earning series. From this perspective, the major research question is whether alternative measures of value added capture dimensions of market risk beyond that captured by earnings or cash flow information.

METHOD

A market risk association test is the object of this chapter. More specifically, a regression model with market risk as the dependent variable and accounting betas as the independent variables is used. The purpose is to examine the incremental explanatory power (of value added versus more conventional accounting risk measures) with respect to the variability in market beta.

Market Beta

The market model was used to derive the empirical estimates of market beta:

$$\tilde{R}_{it} = a_i + \beta_i \tilde{R}_{mt} + \tilde{u}_{it} \tag{1}$$

where

$\tilde{R}_{it}$ = rate of return for security i in period t,

a_i = intercept,

β_i = market beta for security i,

$\tilde{R}_{mt}$ = rate of return on market portfolio (equal or value weighted index), and

$\tilde{u}_{it}$ = disturbance terms with $u(\tilde{u}_{it}) = 0$ and constant variance.

Monthly and annual stock returns over up to 20 years or 240 months were used.

Accounting Beta

For the same period, annual observations were used to estimate accounting betas using the time-series regression

$$\tilde{r}_{it} = a_i + b_i \tilde{r}_{mt} + \tilde{e}_{it} \tag{2}$$

where

$\tilde{r}_{it}$ = an accounting return variable for firm i in period t;

a_i = intercept for firm i;

b_i = accounting beta for firm i;

$\tilde{r}_{mt}$ = market index for accounting returns computed as the simple average of the sample accounting returns, $\tilde{r}_{it}$, in period t; and

$\tilde{e}_{it}$ = disturbance term with $u(e_{it}) = 0$ and constant variance.

Because of the beta estimation errors noted in other studies, two approaches were followed: (1) Vasicek's Bayesian technique[9] was used to adjust the initial estimates of betas at the individual firm level and (2) the analysis was also performed at a four-security-portfolio level (based on a ranking of market beta).

The Bayesian adjustments are done as follows:

$$B* = \frac{B'/vb + B/vb}{1/vb' + 1/vb} \tag{3}$$

where

$B*$ = Bayesian adjusted beta,

B' = prior estimate of beta,

B = firm's (unadjusted) estimate of beta,

vb' = prior estimate of variance beta, and

vb = firm's variance of beta.

This adjustment process is applied cross-sectionally. The priors, B' and vb' of beta are estimated for the sample. Thus a firm's beta is adjusted toward the sample mean beta, weighted by its relative beta variance versus the overall beta variance.

Accounting Return Variables

The accounting return variables used were based on value added, earnings, or cash flow measures. The value added measures were either a

Exhibit 6.1
Value Added Variables: Relationship with Systematic Risk Firms Included in Different Stages of the Analysis

Initial sample of firms identified as reporting labor and related expenses

for 20 years (COMPUSTAT data item 42):	224
Firms missing other COMPUSTAT data:	(82)
Firms having all needed COMPUSTAT data for all 20 years:	135
Firms missing CRSP monthly returns:	(32)
Firms in final sample (with both market and accounting betas):	103

Source: Karpik, P., and A. Belkaoui, "The Relative Relationship between Systematic Risk and Value Added Variables," *Journal of International Financial Management and Accounting* 1, no. 3 (1989): 264. Reprinted with permission.

gross value added or a net value added measure. More explicitly, these measures are defined from Compustat data items as follows:

1. Gross value added (VA) = the sum of labor expenses, corporate taxes, depreciation expenses, dividends, interest expenses, minority interests in subsidiaries + change in retained earnings, divided by the beginning of the period market value of common equity.
2. Net value added (NVA) = the sum of labor expenses, corporate taxes, dividends, interest expenses, minority shareholders in subsidiaries + retained earnings, divided by the beginning of the period market value of common equity.
3. Earnings (E) = income available to common equity divided by the beginning of the period market value of common equity.
4. Cash flow (CF) = cash flows generated from continuing operations divided by beginning of the period market value of equity, where cash flows are defined as income available to common plus depreciation, deferred taxes, and the changes in noncash working capital.

Data Source and Sample Selection

The firms examined in this study represent all NYSE and AMEX firms that have available data over the period 1968–1987. Exhibit 6.1 indicates the number of firms available for each phase of the analysis. The initial sample was identified from Compustat. Missing labor expense data reduced the sample size to 224 firms. Other relevant accounting data that were missing from this study further reduced the sample size to 141 firms. Finally, missing stock returns from CRSP reduced the sample to the final sample of 103 firms. Constructing four-firm portfolios resulted in 26 portfolios.

EMPIRICAL RESULTS

Descriptive Statistics

The means and standard deviations for the market and accounting betas for the 103 single securities and for the 26 four-firm portfolios are shown in Exhibit 6.2. The descriptive statistics for single security betas are first shown unadjusted, then Bayesian adjusted using the Bayesian technique. Two relevant observations may be made. First as found in other studies, relative to betas at the individual firm level, the portfolio analysis generally reduced the variability of betas, especially accounting betas. The Bayesian revision imparts only minor reduction in variability of all betas, probably because of the low mean market beta of the sample (0.68 versus the overall market mean of 1.00). Second, the sample market betas have considerably less variability compared to accounting betas. This is expected due to using a different number of observations for the market beta and annual observations for the accounting betas.

Correlation Results

The Pearson product moment correlations between the individual firm's unadjusted (part 1) betas examined for individual securities Bayesian adjusted (part 2) betas and the four-security-portfolio (part 3) betas are shown in Exhibit 6.3. Several observations may be made.

First, in accord with prior studies, the association between market betas and accounting betas is stronger at the portfolio level than at the single-security level.

Second, with one exception, the association between market betas and value added betas is much greater than between market betas and earnings betas and/or cash flow betas. The net value added beta has the highest average correlation with market risk at both the single-firm level

Exhibit 6.2
Summary Statistics of Market and Accounting Betas

(All Betas based on equal weighted indices using 20 years of data, Market Betas are

monthly and Accounting Betas are annual)

Betas for Single Securities (N=103)

Variable	Description	Mean	Std. Dev.
BETA	MARKET BETA	0.68294913	0.25612288
BM__E	EARNINGS BETA	1.07051947	3.34067355
BM__CF	CASHFLOW BETA	1.05217996	0.93325600
BM__VA	VAL ADDED-GROSS	1.07717130	1.41860854
BM__NVA	VAL ADDED-NET	1.07496015	1.43373869

Bayesian Revised Betas for Single Securities (N=103)

Variable	Description	Mean	Std. Dev.
BBETA	MARKET BETA	0.67624790	0.23251492
BB__E	EARNINGS BETA	1.07099797	3.32827857
BB__CF	CASHFLOW BETA	1.05282488	0.88202439
BB__VA	VAL ADDED-GROSS	1.07828422	1.39950768
BB__NVA	VAL ADDED-NET	1.07599338	1.41388054

Portfolio Betas (N=26)
(Portfolios of four firms ranked by Market Beta)

Variable	Description	Mean	Std. Dev.
PBETA	MARKET BETA	0.68218699	0.25831901
PB__E	EARNINGS BETA	1.07086215	1.04643418
PB__CF	CASHFLOW BETA	1.05363723	0.61070900
PB__VA	VAL ADDED-GROSS	1.07178560	1.18115977
PB__NVA	VAL ADDED-NET	1.06979381	1.20910425

Source: Karpik, P., and A. Belkaoui, "The Relative Relationship between Systematic Risk and Value Added Variables," *Journal of International Financial Management and Accounting* 1, no. 3 (1989): 265. Reprinted with permission.

and the portfolio level. The single exception is the high association between earning beta and market risk at the portfolio level.

Third, relevant to the issue of comparability of value added measures, the association among market betas, earnings betas, and cash flow betas is greater with net value added betas than with gross value added betas. This implies that the accounting measure of depreciation (which differ-

Exhibit 6.3
Pearson Correlation Matrices

Market and Accounting Betas

(All Betas based on equal weighted indices using 20 years of data,

Market Betas are monthly and Accounting Betas are annual)

PEARSON CORRELATION COEFFICIENTS/(PROB> |R| UNDER HO: RHO=0)

Betas for Single Securities (N=103)

Variable/Beta Type	Beta	BM__E	BM__CF	BM__VA
BETA MARKET BETA	1.0			
BM__E BETA EARNINGS	0.22153 (0.0245)	1.0		
BM__CF BETA CASHFLOW	0.18565 (0.0605)	0.60235 (0.0001)	1.0	
BM__VA BETA VAL ADD GROSS	0.51637 (0.0001)	0.19218 (0.0001)	0.63504 (0.0518)	1.0
BM__NVA BETA VAL ADDED NET	0.54538 (0.0001)	0.27381 (0.0051)	0.65386 (0.0001)	0.99511 (0.0001)

Bayesian Revised Betas for Single Securities (N=103)

Variable/Beta type	BBeta	BB__E	BB__CF	BB__VA
BBETA BAYESIAN MKT BETA	1.0			
BB__E BAYESIAN EARNINGS	0.21035 (0.0330)	1.0		
BB__CF BAYESIAN CASHFLOW	0.16057 (0.1052)	0.59769 (0.0001)	1.0	
BB__VA BAYSN VAL ADD-GROSS	0.49172 (0.0001)	0.18831 (0.0568)	0.6335 (0.0001)	1.0
BB__NVA BAYESIAN VAL ADD-NET	0.52083 (0.0001)	0.27015 (0.0058)	0.65195 (0.0001)	0.99511 (0.0001)

Portfolio Betas (N=26)
(Portfolios contain four firms ranked by Market Beta)

Variable/Beta Type	PBeta	PB__E	PB__CF	PB__VA
PBETA PORTFOLIO MKT BETA	1.0			
PB__E PORTFOLIO EARNINGS	0.72847 (0.0001)	1.0		
PB__CF PORTFOLIO CASHFLOW	0.27798 (0.1691)	0.79865 (0.0001)	1.0	
PB__VA PORT VAL ADDED-GROSS	0.60471 (0.0011)	0.93227 (0.0001)	0.84567 (0.0001)	1.0
PB__NVA PORT VAL ADDED-NET	0.63218 (0.0005)	0.94062 (0.0001)	0.83313 (0.0001)	0.99909 (0.0001)

Source: Karpik, P., and A. Belkaoui, "The Relative Relationship between Systematic Risk and Value Added Variables," *Journal of International Financial Management and Accounting* 1, no. 3 (1990): 267. Reprinted with permission.

entiates between gross versus net value added) adds variability that is not associated with market risk. Such a finding is consistent with investors interpreting cross-sectional depreciation differences as poor surrogates of economic depreciation and/or such accounting measures vary because of the different accounting methods used.

Regression Results

Exhibits 6.4, 6.5, and 6.6 show the regression for single securities using adjusted and unadjusted betas and for the four-security-portfolio case. In each case, the dependent variable is the market risk and the independent variables are one, two, or three of the accounting betas. At the single-security level, the highest R^2 values are obtained using the value added betas as independent variables: An R^2 of 0.299 for the gross value added and an R^2 of 0.291 for the net value added. Similarly, in comparing the regressions using a single independent variable of either earnings betas (model 1) or cash flow betas (model 2), with the corresponding regressions where either gross value added betas are included (models 6, 7, 8, and 9) there is a drastic improvement in R^2 from under 5 percent to a high of over 30 percent for model 9. Finally, in comparing model 5, with earnings beta and cash flow beta as independent variables, to models 10 and 11, where the value added betas are included as the third independent variables, there is also a drastic improvement of R^2 from under 5 percent to over 35 percent. In brief, the value added betas have the highest explanatory power, and their addition to models with cash flow betas and earnings betas dramatically increases the overall explanatory power.

The results of the portfolio analysis show a somewhat different picture. The explanatory power of each value added variable is highly significant, although the earnings beta registered the highest R^2. The value added betas still dominate the cash flow beta results and add substantial explanatory power when combined with cash flow betas.

SUMMARY AND DISCUSSIONS

The objective of this chapter was to assess the explanatory power of value added accounting variables relative to and beyond accrual earnings and cash flow variable explanations of market risk (beta). At an individual firm level, both value added betas had a much greater association with market betas than did either earnings or cash flow betas. This was

Exhibit 6.4
Regressions of Market Beta on Accounting Betas I

Single Securities (N=103)
(All Betas based on equal weighted indices using 20 years of data,
Market Betas are monthly and Accounting Betas are annual)

BETA = BETA OF MONTHLY MARKET RETURNS (MARKET VALUE DEFLATED)
BM_E = BETA OF EARNINGS (MARKET VALUE DEFLATED)
BM_CF = BETA OF CASHFLOW (MARKET VALUE DEFLATED)
BM_VA = BETA OF VALUE ADDED GROSS (MARKET VALUE DEFLATED)
BM_NVA= BETA OF VALUE ADDED NET (MARKET VALUE DEFLATED)

MODEL: BETA (MARKET) $= B_0 + B_1(X1) + B_2(X2) + B_3(X3) + B_4(X4)$

Mdl	X1 B_1(t-stat)	X2 B_2(t-stat)	X3 B_3(t-stat)	X4 B_4(t-stat)	R^2	MSE (F-stat)
1.	BM_E 0.017 (2.28)				0.040	0.251 (5.21)
2.	BM_CF 0.051 (1.90)				0.025	0.253 (3.61)
3.	BM_VA 0.093 (6.06)				0.259	0.220 (36.72)
4.	BM_NVA 0.097 (6.54)				0.291	0.216 (42.76)
5.	BM_E 0.013 (1.41)	BM_CF 0.022 (0.67)			0.034	0.252 (2.82)
6.	BM_E 0.010 (1.47)	BM_VA 0.089 (5.70)			0.268	0.219 (19.65)
7.	BM_E 0.006 (0.90)	BM_NVA 0.094 (6.04)			0.289	0.216 (21.74)
8.	BM_CF −0.065 (−2.20)	BM_VA 0.121 (6.17)			0.287	0.216 (21.49)
9.	BM_CF −0.082 (−2.80)	BM_NVA 0.132 (6.94)			0.336	0.209 (26.75)
10.	BM_E 0.031 (4.00)	BM_CF −0.156 (−4.36)	BM_VA 0.144 (7.53)		0.380	0.202 (21.80)
11.	BM_E 0.025 (3.30)	BM_CF −0.148 (−4.31)	BM_NVA 0.144 (7.79)		0.396	0.199 (23.21)
12.	BM_E −0.022 (−1.24)	BM_CF −0.065 (−1.49)	BM_VA −0.976 (−2.92)	BM_NVA 1.100 (3.36)	0.438	0.192 (20.87)

Source: Karpik, P., and A. Belkaoui, "The Relative Relationship between Systematic Risk and Value Added Variables," Journal of International Financial Management and Accounting 1, no. 3 (1990): 268. Reprinted with permission.

Exhibit 6.5
Regressions of Market Beta on Accounting Betas II

Single Security Bayesian Revised Betas (N=103)
(All Betas based on equal weighted indices using 20 years of data,
Market Betas are monthly and Accounting Betas are annual.

BBETA = BAYESIAN BETA OF MONTHLY MARKET RETURNS (DEFLATED)
BB_E   = BAYESIAN BETA OF EARNINGS (DEFLATED)
BB_CF = BAYESIAN BETA OF CASHFLOW (DEFLATED)
BB_VA = BAYESIAN BETA OF VALUE ADDED GROSS (DEFLATED)
BB_NVA = BAYESIAN BETA OF VALUE ADDED NET (DEFLATED)

MODEL: BBETA (MARKET) = $B_0 + B_1(X1) + B_2(X2) + B_3(X3) + B_4(X4)$

Mdl	X1 B_1(t-stat)	X2 B_2(t-stat)	X3 B_3(t-stat)	X4 B_4(t-stat)	R^2	MSE (F-stat)
1.	BBM_E 0.015 (2.16)				0.035	0.052 (4.68)
2.	BBM_CF 0.042 (1.64)				0.016	0.053 (2.67)
3.	BBM_VA 0.082 (5.68)				0.234	0.041 (32.21)
4.	BBM_NVA 0.086 (6.13)				0.264	0.040 (37.60)
5.	BBM_E 0.012 (1.46)	BBM_CF 0.014 (0.45)			0.027	0.053 (2.42)
6.	BBM_E 0.009 (1.39)	BBM_VA 0.078 (5.34)			0.241	0.041 (17.22)
7.	BBM_E -0.005 (0.85)	BBM_NVA 0.082 (5.67)			0.262	0.040 (19.12)
8.	BBM_CF -0.066 (-2.30)	BBM_VA 0.108 (5.94)			0.265	0.40 (19.42)
9.	BBM_CF -0.082 (-2.88)	BBM_NVA 0.119 (6.69)			0.314	0.037 (19.42)
10.	BBM_E 0.29 (3.94)	BBM_CF -0.153 (-4.39)	BBM NVA 0.130 (7.26)		0.358	0.035 (24.29)
11.	BBM_E 0.023 (3.26)	BBM_CF -0.145 (-4.34)	BBM_NVA 0.130 (7.51)		0.374	0.034 (19.99)
12.	BBM_E -0.021 (-1.28)	BBM_CF -0.064 (-1.51)	BBM_VA -0.923 (-2.94)	BBM_NVA 1.034 (3.36)	0.419	0.031 (21.30)

Source: Karpik, P., and A. Belkaoui, "The Relative Relationship between Systematic Risk and Value Added Variables," *Journal of International Financial Management and Accounting* 1, no. 3 (1990): 269. Reprinted with permission.

Exhibit 6.6
Regressions of Market Beta on Accounting Betas III

Portfolios (N=26) of four firms ranked by Market Beta
(All Betas based on equal weighted indices using 20 years of data,
Market Betas are monthly and Accounting Betas are annual)

PBETA = PORTFOLIO BETA OF MONTHLY MARKET RETURNS (DEFLATED)
PB_E = PORTFOLIO BETA OF EARNINGS (DEFLATED)
PB_CF = PORTFOLIO BETA OF CASHFLOW (DEFLATED)
PB_VA = PORTFOLIO BETA OF VALUE ADDED GROSS (DEFLATED)
PB_NVA PORTFOLIO BETA OF VALUE ADDED NET (DEFLATED)

MODEL: $PBETA\ (MARKET) = B_0 + B_1(X1) + B_2(X2) + B_3(X3) + B_4(X4)$

Mdl	X1 B_1(t-stat)	X2 B_2(t-stat)	X3 B_3(t-stat)	X4 B_4(t-stat)	R^2	MSE (F-stat)
1.	PB_E 0.150 (4.60)				0.446	0.029 (27.14)
2.	PB_CF 0.201 (3.11)				0.258	0.039 (2.01)
3.	PB_VA 0.127 (4.22)				0.402	0.031 (13.84)
4.	PB_NVA 0.125 (4.31)				0.413	0.031 (15.98)
5.	PB_E 0.155 (2.80)	PB_CF -0.011 (-0.11)			0.423	0.030 (42.13)
6.	PB_E 0.128 (1.39)	PB_VA 0.021 (0.26)			0.424	0.030 (15.43)
7.	PB_E 0.120 (1.23)	PB_NVA 0.027 (0.32)			0.425	0.030 (14.38)
8.	PB_CF -0.020 (-0.18)	PB_VA 0.135 (2.36)			0.376	0.033 (14.46)
9.	PB_CF -0.017 (-0.16)	PB_NVA 0.132 (2.47)			0.388	0.032 (17.38)
10.	PB_E 0.129 (1.38)	PB_CF -0.028 (-0.26)	PB_VA 0.032 (0.34)		0.400	0.032 (27.03)
11.	PB_E 0.122 (1.22)	PB_CF -0.027 (-0.26)	PB_VA 0.037 (0.39)		0.401	0.032 (27.27)
12.	PB_E 0.064 (0.46)	PB_CF 0.039 (0.26)	PB_VA -0.730 (-0.61)	PB_VA 0.770 (0.64)	0.383	0.032 (27.10)

Source: Karpik, P., and A. Belkaoui, "The Relative Relationship between Systematic Risk and Value Added Variables," Journal of International Financial Management and Accounting 1, no. 3 (1990): 270. Reprinted with permission.

true regardless of whether individual- or multivariable models are examined, or whether unadjusted or Bayesian adjusted variables are used. Thus value added information does provide incremental information relative to earnings or cash flow information in explaining market beta at the individual firm level.

The net version appears marginally superior to the gross version of value added, implying that depreciation expense variations (included in gross) may be ignored. The portfolio level model results show that earnings betas are much more closely related to portfolio market betas than at the individual firm level. The explanatory power of the other variables also improves but to a lesser extent. The general improvement, reduction in mean square error (MSE) and increased R^2 from using portfolio betas versus individual firm betas, results from the increased estimation efficiency.

Portfolio beta findings are more relevant to issues concerning well-diversified security investments. At the portfolio level, all of the accounting betas are significantly associated with market betas, with the earnings betas slightly outperforming the other accounting betas. Risk estimation applications at the firm level, however, deal with greater uncertainly,[10] and it is in these situations that value added betas greatly outperform cash flow and especially earnings betas when explaining market beta variations. These findings are consistent with earnings and cash flows being more transitory than the value added measures relative to market risk. Increasing the size of the portfolios (from four firms in each) would generally increase the association of the accounting betas with market betas, thereby increasing the difference between firm versus portfolio level results. This would not likely affect the firm-level explanatory power of the value added betas relative to the accounting betas.

Generalizations about the study's results are qualified by two factors: (1) whether the sample is representative of a larger population of firms and/or (2) whether the findings are stable over time. Each factor is discussed in turn. First, the representativeness of the sample is indicated by firms studied versus the unselected firms. The firms that disclose labor expenses, a key component of value added accounting measures, are relatively rare and are self-selected. The level of market risk for the sample firms (mean market betas of 0.68) is much less than that of the general market mean of 1.00. The total sample of 103 excludes any firms in the banking or financial services industries, and contains two general types of industrial groups, which have substantially different market beta levels: (1) utilities with 44 firms (mean equal weighted beta of 0.46 and value weighted beta of 0.56) and (2) general industrial and related businesses with 59 firms (mean equal weighted beta of 0.84 and value weighted beta of 1.09). The general group consists of various industries of which the oil and gas industry ($n = 9$) is the single largest; overall, the larger and more successful firms listed on the NYSE are members of the nonutility group. Thus the results may not be generalizable to nonrepresented industries or smaller, riskier, and/or less successful firms. Including nonrepresented firms is not expected to affect the results, but it is an issue worthy of further study.

Second, the analysis covers 20 years and assumes a stable process throughout that period. Ismael and Kim[11] find no material differences between using 10-year subperiods versus 20-year periods for analyzing accounting betas. Their findings are corroborated in the current analysis, which was conducted using market and accounting betas calculated using 10- and 5-year subperiods. Each type of beta was highly consistent both across subperiods and over time. Thus the findings do not appear to be affected by the subperiod definition (betas for 20-, 10-, and 5-year periods are highly correlated) and appear to be stable over time (between each 5- and 10-year period).

CONCLUSIONS

The important policy implication of the study reported in this chapter is that value added accounting information can supply considerable explanatory power of market risk beyond that provided by earnings or cash flow measures, especially at the individual firm level. Thus an important accounting policy issue is whether firms should be required to disclose the underlying data needed to calculate value added variables. The current disclosure system does not mandate the disclosure of some of the information needed to compute the value added. At present, less than 10 percent of the firm listed on Compustat consistently disclose labor expenses, a key variable. The cost of reporting this data should be relatively immaterial given the general availability of such information; firms already process this information for payroll purposes and report such information to various governmental agencies. Given the low cost relative to the potentially much greater benefit shown in this chapter, releasing value added reports or disclosing the underlying data needed to calculate the value added appears to be an improvement over the present U.S reporting system. Whether such disclosures should be mandated by standard-setting establishments is an issue worth considering.

NOTES

1. Ismail, B. E., and M. K. Kim, "On the Association of Cash Flow Variables with Market Risk: Further Evidence," *The Accounting Review* (January 1989): 125–136.

2. Meek, G. K., and S. J. Gray, "The Value Added Statement: An Innovation for U.S. Companies?" *Accounting Horizon* (June 1988): 73–81.

3. Maunders, K. T., "The Decision Relevance of Value Added Reports," in *Frontiers of International Accounting: An Anthology*, ed. F. D. Choi and G. G. Ridder, 205. (Ann Arbor, MI: UMI Research Press, 1985).

4. Ibid., 227–229.

5. Ibid., 228.

6. Beaver, W., and J. Manegold, "The Association between Market-Determined and Accounting Determined Risk Measures," *The Accounting Review* (October 1970): 654–682.

7. Rosenberg, B., and J. Grey, "Prediction of Beta from Investment Fundamentals," *Financial Analysts Journal* (May–June 1976): 1–15.

8. Rosenberg, B., and J. Gray, "Predictions of Beta from Investment Fundamentals: Part Two, Alternative Predictions Method," *Financial Analyst Journal* (July–August 1976): 62–70.

9. Vasicek, O., "A Note on Using Cross-Sectional Information in Bayesian Estimation of Security Betas," *The Journal of Finance* (December 1973): 1233–1239.

10. Foster, G., *Financial Statement Analysis*, 2nd ed. (Englewood Cliffs, NJ: Prentice-Hall, 1986), 355.

11. Ismail and Kim, op. cit.

REFERENCES

Abdel-Khalik, A. R., and T. R. Keller. *Earnings or Cash Flows: An Experiment on Functional Fixation and the Valuation of the Firm.* Studies in Accounting Research. No 16. Saratoga, FL, American Accounting Association, 1979.

Accounting Standards Steering Committee. *The Corporate Report.* London: Accounting Standards Steering Committee, 1975.

Beaver, W. *Financial Reporting: An Accounting Revolution.* Englewood Cliffs, NJ: Prentice-Hall, 1981.

Beaver, W. H., P. Kettler, and M. Scholes. "The Association Between Market Determined and Accounting Determined Risk Measures." *The Accounting Review* (October 1970): 654–682.

Beaver, W., and W. R. Landsman. "Incremental Information Content of Statement 33 Disclosures." Research Report, Financial Accounting Standards Board, 1983.

Beaver, W., and J. Manegold. "The Association between Market-Determined and Accounting Determined Measures of Systematic Risk: Some Further Evidence." *Journal of Financial and Quantitative Analysis* (June 1975): 231–284.

Belkaoui, A. *The New Environment in International Accounting: Issues and Practices.* Westport, CT: Greenwood Press, 1988.

Bernard, V. L., and T. L. Stober. "The Nature and Amount of Information in Cash Flows and Accruals." *The Accounting Review* (October 1989): 624–652.

Blume, M. "On the Assessment of Risk." *Journal of Finance* (March 1971): 1–10.

———. "Betas and Their Regression Tendencies." *Journal of Finance* (June 1975): 785–895.

Bowman, R. G. "The Theoretical Relationship Between Systematic Risk and Financial (Accounting) Variables." *Journal of Finance* (June 1979): 617–630.

———. "The Debt Equivalence of Leases: An Empirical Investigation." *The Accounting Review* (April 1980): 237–253.

Cox, B. *Value Added: An Appreciation for the Accounts Concerned with Industry.* London: Heinemann, 1978.

Fama, E. F., and J. MacBeth. "Risk, Return, and Equilibrium: Empirical Tests." *Journal of Political Economy* (May–June 1973): 607–636.

Foster, G. *Financial Statement Analysis.* 2nd ed. (Englewood Cliffs, NJ: Prentice-Hall, 1986).

Gray, S. J., and K. T. Maunders. *Value Added Reporting: Uses and Measurement.* London: Association of Certified Accountants, 1980.

Hamada, R. S. "The Effect of the Firm's Capital Structure on the Systematic Risk of Common Stocks." *Journal of Finance* (May 1972): 435–452.

Harris, G. J. "Value Added Statements." *The Australian Accountant* (May 1982): 261–264.

Ismael, B. E., and M. K. Kim. "On the Association of Cash Flow Variables with Market Risk: Further Evidence." *The Accounting Review* (January 1989): 125–136.

Lev, B., and J. A. Ohlson. "Market Based Empirical Research: A Review, Interpretation and Extension." *Journal of Accounting Research* (Supplement 1982): 239–322.

Levy, R. "On the Short-Term Stationarity of Beta Coefficients." *Financial Analysts Journal* (November–December 1971): 55–62.

Maunders, K. T. "The Decision Relevance of Value Added Reports." In *Frontiers of International Accounting: An Anthology,* edited by F. D. Choi and G. G. Mueller, 225–245. Ann Arbor, MI: UMI Research Press, 1985.

McLeary, S. "Value Added: A Comparative Study." *Accounting Organizations and Society* 8, no. 1 (1983): 31–56.

Meek, G. K., and S. J. Gray. "The Value Added Statement: An Innovation for U.S. Companies?" *Accounting Horizon* (June 1988): 73–81.

Morley, M. F. "The Value Added Statement: A British Innovation." *The Chartered Accountant Magazine* (May 1978): 31–34.

———. "The Value Added Statement in Britain." *The Accounting Review* (May 1979): 618–689.

Neter, J., and W. Wasserman. *Applied Linear Statistical Models.* Homewood, IL: Richard D. Irwin, 1974.

Renshall, M., Allan, R., and K. Nicholson. *Added Value in External Financial Reporting.* London: Institute of Chartered Accountants in England and Wales, 1979.

Rosenberg, B., and J. Grey, "Prediction of Beta from Investment Fundamentals." *Financial Analysts Journal* (May–June 1976): 1–15 and (July–August 1976): 1–11.

Rosenberg, B., and J. Grey. "Predictions of Beta from Investment Fundamentals: Part Two, Alternative Predictions Method." *Financial Analyst Journal* (July–August 1976): 62–70.

Rutherford, B. A. "Value Added as a Focus of Attention for Financial Reporting: Some Conceptual Problems." *Accounting and Business Research* (Summer 1972): 215–220.

———. "Published Statements of Value Added: A Study of Three Years' Experience." *Accounting and Business Research* (Winter 1980): 15–28.

Sinha, G. *Value Added Income.* Calcutta: Book World, 1983.

Suojanen, W. W. "Accounting Today and the Large Corporations." *The Accounting Review* (July 1954): 391–398.

Vasicek, O. "A Note on Using Cross-Sectional Information in Bayesian Estimation of Security Betas." *The Journal of Finance* (December 1973): 1233–1239.

Wilson, G. P. "The Relative Information Content of the Accruals and Cash Flows: Combined Evidence at the Earnings Announcement and Annual Report Release Date." *Journal of Accounting Research* (Supplement 1986): 165–200.

———. "The Incremental Information Content of the Accrual and Funds Components of Earnings after Controlling for Earnings." *The Accounting Review* (April 1987): 293–322.

Chapter 7

Takeover and Value Added Variables

INTRODUCTION

Value added represents revenues less costs of materials brought in from external sources. In this sense, value added is a measure of the increase in value from the firm's productive activities before the distribution of funds to groups of stakeholders such as shareholders, bondholders, employees, and government. As such, the magnitude of the firm's value added, relative to its total assets, represents a measure of the firm's ability to efficiently generate value to distribute to stakeholders. Firms that have a low value added to total assets ratio may thus be viewed as less efficient than other firms and may become candidates for a merger.

This chapter examines the relationship between merged firms and their premerger industries and finds that, in a sample of 234 completed mergers over the period 1977–1989, acquired firms have mean and median value added to total assets ratios below their industry means and medians in the year preceding the year of the takeover. Exhibit 7.1 shows a frequency distribution for the sample by the year of Compustat delisting. If value added is interpreted as a measure of managerial performance

Portions of Chapter 7 are adapted from: Bannister, James W., and Ahmed Riahi-Belkaoui, "Value Added and Corporate Control in the U.S.," *Journal of International Financial Management and Accounting* 3, no. 3 (1991): 241–257. Reprinted with permission.

Exhibit 7.1
Frequency Distribution of the Sample by Year of Compustat Delisting

Year of delisting	Number of targets
1977	11
1978	14
1979	20
1980	18
1981	19
1982	19
1983	19
1984	19
1985	17
1986	22
1987	23
1988	22
1989	11
Total	234

Source: Bannister, James W., and Ahmed Riahu-Belkaoui, "Value Added and Corporate Control in the U.S.," *Journal of International Financial Management and Accounting* 3, no. 3 (1991): 247. Reprinted with permission.

before reinvestment and distributions to shareholders, bondholders, government, and employees, the implication is that target firms were underperformers, which may have been taken over for a better use of their asset potential.

Further, in a subsample of firms with sufficient data for an abnormal return analysis, a cross-sectional regression of cumulative abnormal returns on takeover characteristics and the difference between target firm and average premerger industry value added to total assets indicates that the difference in value added ratios has significant explanatory power. The implication is that the value added to total assets of acquired firms relative to the average for their industries is positively related to the value created for their stockholders during the takeover. As value added to total assets less industry average value added to total assets increases, greater abnormal returns are observed. These two results suggest that value added is a measure of return which has economic relevance in the analysis of takeovers.

TAKEOVER BIDS AND THE VALUE ADDED TO TOTAL ASSETS RATIO

Lev[1] reviews theories and empirical evidence related to rationales for mergers and suggests that a major cause of takeover bids is target firm undervaluation (or underperformance) and/or managerial motives. Further, Coffee[2] suggests that a cause for market undervaluation leading to takeover is the failure of management to efficiently manage the firms' assets. Management underperformance could result from either the failure to recognize the best use of invested capital or from managers' tendency to avoid risk in order to protect their personal human capital investment in the firm. Thus, takeovers may be motivated by the bidder's desire to acquire an inefficiently managed firm, displace inferior managers, and benefit from the existing disparity between the target's actual and potential market values. If target firms are undervalued in the capital market due to underperformance, and this underperformance is represented by the firm's accounting measures of return, then the ratio of value added to total assets provides a set of empirical predictions concerning the sources of value in takeovers and the characteristics of takeover targets. Accordingly, the following hypothesis (alternative form) is tested:

H_1: The value added to total assets ratio of target firms is less than the average value added to total assets ratio in the target firm's industry.

This hypothesis is tested by comparing the mean and median of differences in target firm versus average premerger industry value added to total assets.

An additional issue of interest is the extent to which acquiring firms value the available return of target firms (as measured by value added to total assets). As indicated later, value added is an accounting measure of the firm's total return before allocation to stakeholder groups. The way that this total return is allocated among the various stakeholder groups is, in part, a management decision relating a particular view of the contributions of each group. Other things being equal, if target firms have larger (smaller) value added per dollar of total assets than other firms in their industry, then more (less) value exists to be redistributed under new management. Further, given that takeovers are costly, acquiring firms are likely to value the ability to have immediate access to existing resources.

Under this scenario, the position of the target firm's value added to total assets relative to the standard in its industry should proxy the extent to which an acquiring firm can exploit the resources of the target firm. As a consequence, it should be positively related to the price that a bidding firm will pay for a target and, thus, the abnormal returns accruing to the target firm's shareholders. Let DVA be equal to the target firm's value added (gross or net) to total assets ratio less the average comparable ratio for its industry. Then the second hypothesis is

H_2: DVA is positively related to target firm cumulative abnormal returns observed during the interval from the first announcement of a takeover offer to the date of takeover resolution.

To analyze the extent to which DVA can explain abnormal returns to targets, the regression in equation (1) below is estimated:

$$CAR = a_0 + a_1 DVA \qquad (1)$$

where CAR is the cumulative abnormal return of the target over the takeover contest period and DVA is as previously defined.

A number of additional factors are known to influence the magnitude of target firm abnormal returns during the course of a takeover contest. These factors may confound the results of the analysis of DVA and are thus controlled for in an additional cross-sectional analysis. First, Huang and Walkling[3] report that returns to target shareholders are higher when the target's management opposes the takeover, and that more wealth is created in cash transactions than in takeovers conducted completely or primarily by the exchange of securities. Further, Servaes[4] reports that the presence of multiple bidders in a takeover increases the return to target firm shareholders. Finally, Bradley et al.[5] note that with the appearance of investment banking firms specializing in takeover financing and the creation of antitakeover devices, the overall merger environment has changed since 1981. This suggests that the costs of mergers and the potential returns to target firm shareholders may have changed over time. Each of these factors may influence the abnormal returns observed during the takeover period and thus confound the test of H_2. Equation (2) presents a model that controls for these confounding factors:

$$CAR = b_0 + b_1 DVA + b_2 CASH + b_3 HF \\ + b_4 BIDS + b_5 AFT80 + b_6 SIZE \qquad (2)$$

where CAR and DVA retain their previous definitions. The control variables have the following definitions: CASH is an indicator variable equaling 1 if the takeover is primarily for cash, and 0 otherwise; HF is

Exhibit 7.2
Frequency of Takeovers Classified by Form of Payment, Hostile or Friendly Offer, and Number of Bidders for the Target[a]

Form of payment[b]	Number of firms	Percent
Cash Payment	44	57.1
Securities	18	23.4
Mixed cash and securities	14	18.2
Form of Payment unknown	1	1.3
Total	77	100.0

Management reaction to offer[c]	Number of firms	Percent
Hostile acquisition	26	33.8
Friendly acquisition	51	66.2
Total	77	100.0

Number of bidders[d]	Number of firms	Percent
1 bidder	54	70.1
2 bidders	15	19.5
3 bidders	5	6.5
4 bidders	3	3.9
Total	77	100.0

[a] Takeover characteristics are reported for the subsample of firms which are covered by CRSP, have an identifiable offer date in the *Wall Street Journal Index* (WSJI), and have target and industry value added data for at least one SIC code level (2, 3, or 4-digit) in at least one of the three years preceding takeover resolution.
[b] Form of compensation as reported in the WSJI and/or the *Mergers and Acquisitions* M&A Roster (M&A).
[c] Takeovers are assumed to be friendly unless the WSJI or M&A report the opposition of target firm management.
[d] Number of firms bidding for the target as reported in the WSJI.

Source: Bannister, James W., and Ahmed Riahu-Belkaoui, "Value Added and Corporate Control in the U.S.," *Journal of International Financial Management and Accounting* 3, no. 3 (1991): 248. Reprinted with permission.

an indicator variable equaling 1 if management's reaction to the takeover indicates that it is hostile, and 0 if friendly; BIDS is an indicator variable equaling 1 if there is more than one bidder for the target, and 0 if there is only one bidder; AFT80 is an indicator variable equaling 1 if the merger occurred after 1980, and 0 if the merger occurred during or before 1980; and, SIZE is the natural logarithm of target firm total assets at the beginning of the year prior to the year that the first takeover offer is announced. Exhibit 7.2 discusses frequency of takeovers by form of payment, whether takeovers were friendly or hostile, and how many bidders there were.

The expectation for DVA remains the same. Given the preceding discussion, the coefficients for CASH, HF, and BIDS are expected to be positive. Because AFT80 and SIZE are included as general control variables, there is no directional expectation for their coefficients.

SAMPLE SELECTION

The Compustat Research File was searched for firms that (1) were delisted due to merger or acquisition over the period 1977–1989 and (2) reported sufficient data to calculate value added in at least one of the three fiscal years prior to the delisting date. Firms listed on the Compustat Primary, Secondary, and Tertiary File, the Full Coverage File, and the Research File were used to construct two-, three-, and four-digit SIC code industry average value added. Two hundred forty-eight firms with sufficient data to calculate value added were delisted from Compustat due to merger or acquisition. However, for 14 of these firms, it was not possible to compute a two-, three-, or four-digit industry average value added for any of the three years preceding Compustat delisting. Thus, the final sample for tests of H_1 consists of 234 firms, which represent 92 four-digit industries. Exhibit 7.1 presents the distribution of the sample by year of Compustat delisting. The distribution over the sample years is reasonably uniform, ranging from 17 to 23 delisting between the years 1979 and 1988, and 11 to 14 delistings in 1977–1978 and 1989.

To be included in the abnormal return analysis (H_2) firms were additionally required to (1) be in an unregulated industry, (2) have an identifiable merger offer date reported in the *Wall Street Journal Index* (WSJI), and (3) have security return data on the CRSP Daily Return File. Other information collected includes (1) the number of bidding firms reported in the WSJI, (2) the form of payment for the merger compensation (cash, securities, or mixed cash and securities) reported in the WSJI or the *Mergers and Acquisitions* M&A Roster (M&A), and (3) the nature of the takeover (friendly or hostile). The takeover was recorded as friendly unless the WSJI or M&A reported that the target management opposed one or more of the offers issued between the date of the first offer and the resolution of the takeover. One hundred and twenty-six of the 234 firms were in unregulated industries. Seventy-seven of the 126 unregulated firms had identifiable merger offer dates and were covered by CRSP. Characteristics of these 77 takeovers are reported in Exhibit 7.2. Most of the takeovers were for cash (57.1%), were friendly acquisitions (66.2%), and had only one bidder (70.1%).

THE VALUE ADDED RATIOS OF TARGET FIRMS
AND THEIR INDUSTRIES

The first hypothesis states that the value added to total assets ratios of target firms is less than the comparable ratios typical to their industries. To test H_1, mean and median ratios of targets and their industry averages are compared for the three years prior to takeover resolution. The variables for the tests are constructed as follows. Gross and net value added (GVA and NVA, respectively) for target firms and industry members are constructed similarly to the right-hand sides of equations (1) and (2). Target firm and industry GVA and NVA are then standardized by beginning-of-period total assets to form gross and net value added to total assets (GVA/TA and NVA/TA, respectively). Average GVA/TA and NVA/TA are then computed for the two-, three-, and four-digit SIC code industries of the target firms. Value added ratios for the target firms are then compared to those in their two-, three-, and four-digit industries.

Exhibit 7.3 reports the comparisons of target firm and industry average GVA/TA and NVA/TA. The results indicate that target firms have significantly lower value added ratios than the other firms in their industries in year $t - 1$, the year preceding the year in which the takeover is completed. For example, at the four-digit SIC code level (panel A), target firms have mean GVA/TA and 0.399 in year $t - 1$. The comparative industry mean is 0.448. Similarly, target firms have mean NVA/TA of 0.349 one year prior to takeover resolution. The comparative industry mean is 0.399. This relationship is also observed when industry is defined at the three- and two-digit SIC code levels (panels B and C, respectively). Similar results are observed in median comparisons, as evidenced by the results of the sign rank tests, and in sign tests. Both the mean and median GVA/TA and NVA/TA of target firms are lower than those of other firms in their industries.

Further, an examination of the number of positive and negative differences for the value added ratios at the four-digit industry level indicates that target firm performance eroded over the three years prior to takeover resolution. More target firms performed above their industry average than below it in year $t - 3$, in year $t - 2$ more target firms were below the industry average than above it, and a significantly greater number of firms were below the industry average than above it in year $t - 1$. Steadily declining performance is also observed at the three-digit industry level, concluding with a significant difference ($x = 0.05$) in year

Exhibit 7.3
Comparison of Target Firm and Average Target Industry Value Added to Total Assets Ratios

Panel A: Industry is defined at the four-digit SIC code level

Year	Var.	n	Target Firm mean	Target Firm median	Target Industry mean	Target Industry median	t-stat[b]	Sign Rank[b]	Sign test pos(neg)
t−3[a]	NVA/TA	140	0.459	0.357	0.436	0.374	0.96	562	75(65)
	GVA/TA	140	0.509	0.434	0.489	0.433	0.85	671	75(65)
t−2	NVA/TA	146	0.445	0.334	0.471	0.401	−0.93	−266	69(77)
	GVA/TA	146	0.501	0.399	0.520	0.436	−0.70	−187	70(76)
t−1	NVA/TA	110	0.349	0.300	0.399	0.336	−1.95**	−716**	45(65)**
	GVA/TA	110	0.399	0.357	0.448	0.386	−1.92**	−688**	43(67)**

Panel B: Industry is defined at the three-digit SIC code level

Year	Var.	n	Target Firm mean	Target Firm median	Target Industry mean	Target Industry median	t-stat[b]	Sign Rank[b]	Sign test pos(neg)
t−3[a]	NVA/TA	158	0.464	0.363	0.445	0.392	0.91	359	80(78)
	GVA/TA	158	0.513	0.434	0.496	0.454	0.78	434	80(78)
t−2	NVA/TA	161	0.448	0.345	0.446	0.384	0.10	−18	78(83)
	GVA/TA	161	0.502	0.399	0.495	0.418	0.33	5	78(83)
t−1	NVA/TA	122	0.365	0.314	0.426	0.375	−2.14**	−825**	48(74)**
	GVA/TA	122	0.414	0.363	0.476	0.394	−2.14**	−791**	48(74)**

Panel C: Industry is defined at the two-digit SIC code level

Year	Var.	n	Target Firm mean	Target Firm median	Target Industry mean	Target Industry median	t-stat[b]	Sign Rank[b]	Sign test pos(neg)
t−3[a]	NVA/TA	190	0.488	0.411	0.482	0.473	0.26	−122	88(102)
	GVA/TA	190	0.536	0.472	0.532	0.516	0.19	−94	90(100)
t−2	NVA/TA	192	0.446	0.390	0.481	0.443	−1.45*	−944	87(105)
	GVA/TA	192	0.498	0.445	0.530	0.494	−1.28*	−862	83(109)*
t−1	NVA/TA	138	0.405	0.336	0.446	0.413	−1.48*	−709*	56(82)**
	GVA/TA	138	0.453	0.385	0.496	0.444	−1.52*	−679*	58(80)*

[a]Year t−1 represents the ith complete fiscal year prior to the resolution of the takeover.

[b]Student's t and sign rank tests are one-tailed. Under the alternative hypothesis, the expected sign in each case is negative. Sign tests are two-tailed.

*Significant at $\alpha \leq 0.10$.

**Significant at $\alpha \leq 0.05$.

***Significant at $\alpha \leq 0.01$.

Source: Bannister, James W., and Ahmed Riahu-Belkaoui, "Value Added and Corporate Control in the U.S.," *Journal of International Financial Management and Accounting* 3, no. 3 (1991): 250. Reprinted with permission.

$t - 1$, and at the two-digit industry level, where differences significant at $x = 0.10$ are observed in years $t - 2$ and $t - 1$.

VALUE ADDED AND TARGET FIRM ABNORMAL RETURNS

The second hypothesis of the paper states that DVA, the difference between target firm and industry average value added is positively related to CAR. This hypothesis is tested by the regressions represented in equations (1) and (2) in an earlier section.

Cumulative abnormal returns for the test of H_2 were constructed as follows: Target firms stocks returns were predicted by the market model.

$$\tilde{R}_{js} = \alpha_j + \beta_j \tilde{R}_{ms} + \tilde{e}_{js}$$

where $\tilde{R}_{js}$ is the daily return for security j on day s, $\tilde{R}_{ms}$ is the CRSP value weighted return on the market on day s, $\tilde{e}_{js}$ is a normally distributed error term, and α_j and β_j are firm-specific parameters to be estimated. Parameters for the market model were estimated over the period ranging from days -209 to -10 relative to the date on which a merger offer announcement was first reported in the WSJI (day $()$). Daily abnormal returns for firm j, AR_{jd} are the market model prediction errors for each day (d) in the cumulation period:

$$AR_{jd} = \tilde{R}_{jd} - (\hat{\alpha}_j + \hat{\beta}_j \tilde{R}_{md})$$

Finally, the AR_{jd} are cumulated to form CAR. The cumulation period is from day -1 relative to the first report of a merger offer announcement in the WSJI, to the date of shareholder approval of the merger.

Seventy-seven firms had identifiable merger offer dates, were covered by CRSP, and had value added data for year $t - 1$, $t - 2$, or $t - 3$ at one or more of the two-, three-, or four-digit industry levels. Mean cumulative abnormal returns for these 77 target firms were 21.96 percent, which is consistent with the findings from previous research.[6]

DVA is constructed as target firm NVA/TA for year $t - 1$ less industry average NVA/TA for year $t - 1$ (where year t is the year that the takeover is completed). DVA is separately computed for industries defined at the two-, three-, and four-digit SIC code levels. The control variables (CASH, HF, BIDS, AFT80, and SIZE) were already defined. The results of the cross-sectional regressions using DVA at the four-digit SIC code level are shown in Exhibit 7.4. Column [1] contains the results of the regression without control variables (see equation [1]). In the absence of control for the characteristics of the takeover, no relationship between CAR and DVA is observed.

Column [2] shows the results of the regression including the control variables (equation [2]). After controlling for target firm size and the characteristics of the takeover, the coefficient for DVA is significantly positive. In the cross section, as the difference between NVA/TA and industry average NVA/TA rises, higher abnormal returns are observed. This is consistent with the notion that the value created for target firm shareholders from merger and acquisition bids is higher as the target firm's net value added increases relative to the average for its industry.

As suggested by prior research, the coefficients for CASH and BIDS are positive and significant, indicating that more value is created for target firm shareholders in takeovers where the payment is primarily in cash (28% higher) and when multiple firms bid for the target (35% higher).

AFT80 has a negative coefficient (significant at $\alpha = 0.10$), indicating that, in this sample, post-1980 mergers created less value for target firm stockholders. This may have been due to management resistance or higher average takeover costs. The coefficients for HF and SIZE are not significant.

Of the 77 firms with sufficient return data and WSJI and M&A coverage, only 19 are in four-digit SIC code industries that have enough firms (three or more) to compute an industry average value added for year $t - 1$. In a second analysis, the definition of DVA is modified in an attempt to increase the number of firms available for tests of H_2. In this analysis, DVA is defined as the difference between target firm and four-digit industry average NVA/TA for year $t - 1$ if target firm and industry data are available. If NVA/TA data are not available for year $t - 1$, then DVA is the difference between target firm and industry average NVA/TA for year $t - 2$. This increases the sample size to 35 observations for the regression with control variables.

The results of regression using the second definition of DVA are reported in Exhibit 7.5. Overall, the results are similar to those reported in Exhibit 7.4. When CAR is regressed on DVA without controlling for takeover characteristics (column [1]), the coefficient for DVA is statistically insignificant. When the control variables are included (column [2]), the coefficients for DVA and BIDS are positive and significant (0.05). The coefficients for AFT80 and CASH are negative and positive,

Exhibit 7.4
Ordinary Least-Squares Regression of CAR or DVA with and without Control Variables Related to Target Firm and Merger Characteristics ($n = 19$)[a]

	[1]	[2]
Intercept[b]	0.177 (3.11)***	0.024 (0.13)
DVA	0.235 (0.84)	0.951 (2.27)**
AFT80		−0.454 (−1.95)*
HF		0.020 (0.10)
CASH		0.276 (2.54)**
BIDS		0.346 (2.66)**
SIZE		0.026 (0.64)
F	0.707 (0.41)	2.608 (0.07)
Adj. R^2 (in %)	−1.65	34.89

[a]DVA is target firm net value added to total assets less average net value added to total assets for the target's four-digit industry. DVA is calculated from data for the last fiscal year prior to takeover resolution (year $t - 1$). The indicator variables are: AFT80 = 1 if the merger takes place after 1980; HF = 1 if the merger is hostile; CASH = 1 if the merger is for cash; BIDS = 1 if there is more than one bidder for the target. SIZE is the natural logarithm of target firm total assets at the beginning of the last year prior to the first takeover offer. CAR is cumulated from the offer date to the date of target firm shareholder approval or exchange delisting, whichever is earlier. The offer date is the date of the first announcement of an offer for the target firm in the takeover contest, it is not necessarily the date of the first offer from the eventual acquiror.

[b]Figures reported for regression variables are coefficient (t statistic). Figures reported for F are F statistic (F probability).

* Significant at $\alpha \leq 0.10$, two-tailed test.
** Significant at $\alpha \leq 0.05$, two-tailed test.
***Significant at $\alpha \leq 0.01$, two-tailed test.

Source: Bannister, James W., and Ahmed Riahu-Belkaoui, "Value Added and Corporate Control in the U.S.," *Journal of International Financial Management and Accounting* 3, no. 3 (1991): 253. Reprinted with permission.

respectively, but are significant only at the $\alpha = 0.10$ level. The coefficients for HF and SIZE remain insignificant.

CONCLUSIONS

The results of this chapter indicate that, first, takeover target firms have lower mean and median value added to total assets ratios than the average in their industries in the year preceding the resolution of the takeover. This suggests that, on average, target firms perform at a level

Exhibit 7.5
Ordinary Least-Squares Regression of CAR or DVA with and without Control Variables Related to Target Firm and Merger Characteristics: DVA Calculated from Data in Years $t - 1$ and $t - 2$[a]

	[1]	[2]
Intercept[b]	0.163 (3.62)***	0.169 (1.08)
DVA	0.127 (0.72)	0.681 (2.37)**
AFT80		−0.232 (−1.76)*
HF		0.104 (0.85)
CASH		0.184 (1.92)*
BIDS		0.296 (3.06)***
SIZE		−0.010 (−0.36)
F	0.521 (0.48)	2.925 (0.03)
Adj. R^2 (in %)	−1.43	29.96
n	35	28

[a]DVA is target firm net value added to total assets less average net value added to total assets for its four-digit industry. DVA is calculated from data for the year $t - 1$, if $t - 1$ data is not available, year $t - 2$ data is used. The indicator variables are: AFT80 = 1 if the merger takes place after 1980; HF = 1 if the merger is hostile; CASH = 1 if the merger is for cash; BIDS = 1 if there is more than one bidder for the target. SIZE is the natural logarithm of target firm total assets at the beginning of the last year prior to the first takeover offer. CAR is cumulated from the offer date to the date of target firm shareholder approval or exchange delisting, whichever is earlier. The offer date is the date of the first announcement of an offer for the target firm in the takeover contest, it is not necessarily the date of the first offer from the eventual acquirer.
[b]Figures reported for regression variables are coefficient (t statistic); for F, F statistic (F probability); for n, number of cross-sectional observations.
*Significant at $\alpha \leq 0.10$, two-tailed test.
**Significant at $\alpha \leq 0.05$, two-tailed test.
***Significant at $\alpha \leq 0.01$, two-tailed test.

Source: Bannister, James W., and Ahmed Riahu-Belkaoui, "Value Added and Corporate Control in the U.S.," *Journal of International Financial Management and Accounting* 3, no. 3 (1991): 235. Reprinted with permission.

below that of other firms in their industries. This adds to the empirical evidence on target firm undervaluation and underperformance as measured by other accounting and market based variables.

Second, the abnormal returns accruing to target firm shareholders increase significantly in the cross section as the difference between target firm net value added to total assets and industry average net value added to total assets increases. This indicates that, in the cross section of target firms, as performance increases relative to the industry, the takeover period gains for target firm shareholders are higher. Firms with higher value added to total assets have more total return to distribute among stakeholders and, as a result, generate greater abnormal returns in a takeover. Target firm abnormal returns are also higher when the takeover is completed for cash and when there are multiple bidders for the target. Taken as a whole, the results of the chapter indicate that value added is worthy of consideration as a tool for the evaluation of the performance of the firm. Although valued added is not a mandatory disclosure in the United States, companies disclosing sufficient information to compute value added allow financial statement users to assess the performance of the firm in ways that differ from traditional assessments based on the balance sheet and income statement. Two caveats, however, apply to the conclusions of this study. First, the sample firms voluntarily reported information sufficient to compute value added and thus may not be representative of all firms. Second, data requirements greatly reduced the sample size available for the abnormal return analysis, which indicates caution in generalizing the abnormal return results to include all mergers and acquisitions.[7]

The FASB's *Statement of Financial Accounting Concepts No. 5* notes that supplementary financial statements can be useful for introducing and gaining experience with new kinds of information. Value added is one such type of information. The American Accounting Association Committee on Accounting and Auditing Measurement[8] has recommended that value added be considered for mandatory disclosure. More research is needed on the relationship of value added data to traditional measures of financial performance as they relate to economic events affecting the firm. Such research may indicate that the value added statement, or mandatory disclosure sufficient to construct a value added statement, would be a desirable addition to the annual reports of U.S. firms.

NOTES

1. Lev, B., "Observations on the Merger Phenomenon and a Review of the Evidence," *Midland Corporate Finance Journal* (Winter 1983): 6–28.

2. Coffee, J. C., "Shareholders Versus Managers: The Strain in the Corporate Web," *Knights, Raiders, and Targets: The Impact of the Hostile Takeover,* ed. J. C. Coffee et al. (Oxford University Press, 1988).

3. Huang, Y., and R. A. Walkling, "Target Abnormal Returns Associated with Acquisition Announcements: Payment, Acquisition Form, and Managerial Resistance," *Journal of Financial Economics* 19 (1987): 329–345.

4. Servaes, H., "Tobin's Q and the Gains from Takeovers," *The Journal of Finance* (March 1991): 409–419.

5. Bradley, M., A. Desai, and E. H. Kim, "Synergistic Gains from Corporate Acquisitions and Their Division Between Stockholders of Target and Acquiring Firms," *Journal of Financial Economics* 91 (1988): 3–40.

6. Dennis, D. K., and J. J. McConnelly, "Corporate Mergers and Security Returns," *Journal of Financial Economics* 16 (1986): 143–187.

7. Financial Accounting Standards Board, *Statements of Financial Accounting Concepts No. 5: Recognition and Measurement in Financial Statements of Business Enterprises* (Stamford, CT: FASB, 1984).

8. American Accounting Association, "Committee on Accounting and Auditing Measurement, 1989–1990," *Accounting Horizons* (September 1991): 81–105.

REFERENCES

Accounting Standards Committee. *The Corporate Report*. London: Accounting Standards Committee, 1975.

American Accounting Association. "Committee on Accounting and Auditing Measurement, 1989–1990." *Accounting Horizons* (September 1991): 81–105.

Belsley, D., E. Kuh, and R. Welsh. *Regression Diagnostics: Identifying Influential Data and Sources of Collinearity*. New York: John Wiley & Sons, 1980.

Bradley, M., A. Desai, and E. H. Kim. "Synergistic Gains from Corporate Acquisitions and Their Division Between Stockholders of Target and Acquiring Firms." *Journal of Financial Economics* 91 (1988): 3–40.

Castagna, A. D., and Z. P. Matoley. "Financial Ratios as Predictors of Company Acquisitions." *Journal of the Securities Institute of Australia* (December 1976): 6–10.

Coffee, J. C. "Shareholders Versus Managers: The Strain in the Corporate Web." In *Knights, Raiders, and Targets: The Impact of the Hostile Takeover*, edited by J. C. Coffee et al. Oxford University Press, 1988.

Cox, B. *Value Added: An Appreciation for the Accounts Concerned with Industry*. London: Heinemann, 1978.

Dennis, D. K., and J. J. McConnelly. "Corporate Mergers and Security Returns." *Journal of Financial Economics* 16 (1986): 143–187.

Financial Accounting Standards Board. *Statements of Financial Accounting Concepts No. 5: Recognition and Measurement in Financial Statements of Business Enterprises*. Stamford, CT: FASB, 1984.

Gray, S. J., and K. T. Maunders. "Recent Developments in Value Added Disclosures." *Certified Accountant* (August 1979): 255–256.

Harris, G. J. "Value Added Statements." *The Australian Accountant* (May 1982): 261–264.

Hasbrouck, J. "The Characteristics of Takeover Targets: q and Other Measures." *Journal of Banking and Finance* 9 (1985): 351–362.

Huang, Y., and R. A. Walkling. "Target Abnormal Returns Associated with Acquisition Announcements: Payment, Acquisition Form, and Managerial Resistance." *Journal of Financial Economics* 19 (1987): 329–345.

Jensen, M. C. "Agency Costs of Free Cash Flow, Corporate Finance and Takeovers." *American Economics Review* 76 (1986): 323–329.

Lang, L., R. Stulz, and R. A. Walkling. "Managerial Performance, Tobins q and the Gains from Successful Tender Offers." *Journal of Financial Economics* 24 (1989): 137–154.

Lev, B. "Observations on the Merger Phenomenon and a Review of the Evidence." *Midland Corporate Finance Journal* (Winter 1983): 6–28.

McLeary, S. "Value Added: A Comparative Study." *Accounting Organizations and Society* 8, no. 1 (1983): 31–56.

Meek, G. K., and S. J. Gray. "The Value Added Statement: An Innovation for U.S. Companies?" *Accounting Horizons* (June 1988): 73–81.

———. "Value Added Reporting." In *Developments in Financial Reporting*, edited by T. Lee, 251–269. London: Philip Allan, 1981.

Morley, M. F. *The Value Added Statement*. London: Gee & Co. for the Institute of Chartered Accountants of Scotland, 1978.

———. "The Value Added Statement in Britain." *Accounting Review* (July 1979): 618–689.

Palepu, K. G. "Predicting Takeover Targets." *Journal of Accounting and Economics* 8 (1986): 3–35.

Renshall, M., R. Allan, and K. Nicholson. *Added Value in External Financial Reporting*. London: Institute of Chartered Accountants in England and Wales, 1979.

Rutherford, B. A. "Published Statements of Value Added: A Study of Three Years' Experience." *Accounting and Business Research* (Winter 1980): 15–28.

Servaes, H. "Tobin's Q and the Gaines from Takeovers." *The Journal of Finance* (March 1991): 409–419.

Simkowitz, M., and R. J. Monroe. "A Discriminant Analysis Function for Conglomerate Targets." *Southern Journal of Business* (November 1971): 1–16.

Stevens, D. L. "Financial Characteristics of Merged Firms: A Multivariate Analysis." *Journal of Financial and Quantitive Analysis* 8 (1973): 149–165.

Chapter 8

The Effects of Ownership Structure on Earnings and Value Added Performance

INTRODUCTION

This chapter develops and tests a model that describes the influence of ownership structure and diversification on earnings-based performance, and the influence of ownership structure on value added–based performance.

EARNINGS BASED ON PERFORMANCE

The separation of ownership and control in the large corporation causes owners' motivations to differ from those of managers.[1] The debate on the importance of stock ownership led one school of thought to argue that the distribution of ownership has important implications for corporate efficiency and strategic development,[2] whereas another argued for the irrelevancy of the distribution of ownership.[3]

Empirical examination of the issue led to conflicting results[4] that were attributed to data problems when attempting to construct meaningful measures of the distribution of stock ownership[5] and performance.[6] The effects of ownership structure on performance are best examined in the

This chapter is adapted from A. Belkaoui and E. Pavik, "The Effect of Ownership Structure and Diversification Strategy in Performance." Copyright © 1992. Reprinted by permission of John Wiley & Sons, Ltd.

context of structural differences between firms, and by developing and testing a model that describes the influence of ownership structure and diversification strategy on performance.

Theoretical Framework

Morck, Schleifer, and Vishny[7] (hereafter MSV) estimated the cross-sectional relationship between stock ownership by the board of directors and corporate performance in 1980 for a sample of 249 *Fortune* 500 firms. Two measures of corporate performance were used: Tobin's Q and the ratio of net cash flows to the replacement cost of capital stock. Unlike Demsetz and Lehn[8] (hereafter DL), MSV relax the assumption of a linear relation between performance and stock ownership, and instead propose a nonmonotonic relationship. They test for different average performance (i.e., regression model intercept) for each of the following categories of board holdings: (1) less than 0.2 percent, (2) between 0.2 percent and 5 percent, (3) between 5 and 20 percent, and (4) greater than 20 percent. They find evidence of a nonmonotonic relationship. Tobin's Q increases, then declines, and finally rises slightly as ownership by the board of directors rises. This chapter expands on MSV along the following lines: First, MSV restricted ownership structure to board ownership as the level of equity ownership of the board of directors. Two different measures of ownership structure–namely, stock concentration and management stockholding—are used here. Second, MSV had one independent variable: ownership structure. Additional independent variables for diversification as measured by related and unrelated diversification are used.

The model, which is illustrated in Exhibit 8.1, indicates that ownership structure as expressed by the degree of stock concentration and management stockholding, and diversification as expressed by the degree of related and unrelated diversification, influence performance as measured by either profit or market capitalization.

Ownership Structure and Performance

Our study differentiates between managers' and stockholders' interests, and views the firm as an imperfect and unstable risk-sharing arrangement among managers, employees, and shareholders that is in flux rather than in equilibrium. The distinction is based on the premise established in the literature on managerial discretion that although stockholders are wealth maximizers requiring a maximization of efficiency,

Exhibit 8.1
Research Model

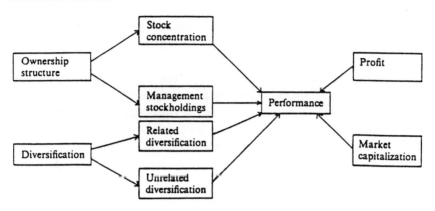

Source: Belkaoui, Ahmed, and Ellen Pavlik, "The Effect of Ownership Structure and Diversification Strategy in Performance," *Managerial and Decision Economics* 13 (1992): 344. Reprinted with permission.

managers have a tendency to maximize personal utility functions that have remuneration, power, security, and status as major factors, requiring a maximization of firm size and diversity.[9] The impact of ownership structure on performance is assumed to differ depending on whether ownership structure is expressed by stock concentration or management stockholding.

Management Stockholding and Performance

Building on the Berle and Means[10] thesis on the deterioration in managerial efficiency associated with the separation of ownership and control characterizing the modern corporation, various theorists have examined the effects of such conflicts of interests on firm performance, and the disciplinary forces that may reduce managers' private returns (e.g., shirking and consumption of perquisites), that is, the market for corporate control,[11] the managerial labor market,[12] incentive contracts,[13] and debt.[14] The empirical evidence of the relationship between firm performance and corporate ownership structure is mixed. Two competing hypotheses characterize this relationship: namely, the convergence-of-interest hypothesis and the entrenchment hypothesis.

According to the convergence-of-interest hypothesis, market value and profitability increase with management ownership. The dispersion of shareholders' ownership allows managers holding little equity in the firm to forego value (wealth) maximization and use corporate assets to benefit themselves rather than the shareholders. Jensen and Meckling[15] argued instead that the costs of deviation from value maximization decline as the manager's stake in the firm rises, because managers are less likely to squander corporate wealth when they bear a larger share of the costs.

According to the entrenchment hypothesis, market value and profitability do not increase with management ownership. Jensen and Meckling[16] pointed out the offsetting costs associated with higher management stockholding. If managers have a small stockholding, they will work toward value maximization as a result of factors including market discipline (e.g., the managerial labor market), the product market,[17] and the market for corporate control.[18] If managers hold a large enough proportion of a firm's stock to have the voting power that guarantees their jobs, they may opt for non-value-maximizing behavior.

What the two hypotheses imply in conjunction with the empirical findings of MSV is that performance will be positively related to lower ranges of management ownership and negatively related to higher ranges of management ownership; in other words, a nonmonotonic relationship is implied.

H_1: There will be a positive (negative) relationship between a firm's performance and management stockholding held at a lower (higher) range.

Stock Concentration and Performance

Shareholders are generally assumed to be value maximizers who view managers' responsibilities to be the maximization of efficiency. With concentrated ownership, stockholders are better able to both coordinate action and demand information that will allow them to overcome any information asymmetry, and influence management's decisions and responsibility toward value maximization and strategies that are in the stockholders' interest. Therefore performance will be negatively related to lower ranges of stock concentration and positively related to higher ranges of stock concentration.

H_2: There will be a negative (positive) relationship between a firm's performance and stock concentration at a lower (higher) range.

Diversification and Performance

Empirical results on the M-Form (Multidivisional Form) hypothesis differentiated between the impact of related diversification and unrelated diversification on performance. In the case of unrelated diversification, managers are thought to trade efficiency for an increase in firm size and decreased operating risks.[19] Empirical evidence shows that unrelated diversification is associated with lower economic returns and lower risk than related diversification. In contrast, both theory and empirical results indicate an association of related diversification with superior economic performance.

H_3: There will be a positive relation between, on the one hand, performance and, on the other, related and unrelated diversification. The relationship will be lower for unrelated diversification as compared to related diversification.

Ownership Structure, Diversification, and Performance

The three hypotheses, H_1, H_2, and H_3, state that performance, as measured by profit or market capitalization, is associated with ownership structure as expressed by the degrees of stock concentration and management stockholding and diversification as expressed by the degrees of related and unrelated diversification. Following the different results obtained by MSV and DL, both piecewise linear regression and strictly linear regression models are tested.

The piecewise linear regression model allowing for two changes in the slope coefficient of stock concentration and management stockholding is used.

The first stage of this analysis starts with turning points of 5 percent and 25 percent for both STC_i and MSH_i following the rationale adopted by MSV. Basically, 5 percent stockholding requires filings on substantial holdings, and 20–30 percent stockholding is considered a deterrent against takeover.

Methods

Dependent Variable

The dependent variable expressing performance of a firm was chosen as either the logarithm of net profit or market capitalization. Market capitalization was computed as the product of the number of shares outstanding and the year-end price per common share. Both variables are highly skewed to the right given their dependence on firm size. The skewness was 2.80591 for profit and 5.1672 for market capitalization. The Kolomogorov D statistic was $D = 0.29003$ (Prob. $> D < 0.01$) for profit and $D = 0.2996$ (Prob. $> D < 0.01$) for market capitalization. If the distribution of the dependent variable is skewed to the right, using a logarithmic transformation helps to normalize it.

Ownership Structure

The data were collected from 1988 proxy statements. Stock concentration was computed as the share of ownership by outside stockholders owning more than 5 percent of the common voting stock in 1987.

Management stockholding were measured by the percentage of common voting stock it held in 1987.

Diversification

The product-count method was used to determine the extent of related and unrelated diversification. The extent of unrelated diversification was measured by the number of two-digit SIC industries outside the primary two-digit industry in which a firm was active during 1987. The extent of related diversification was measured by the number of four-digit SIC industries within its main two-digit industry in which a firm was active during 1987. Dunn and Bradstreet's *Reference Book of Corporate Management* was used to collect the data.

Sample

To ensure a large sample size with readily available data, the initial sample chosen was the *Fortune* 500 industrial corporations; the information needed was gathered from the Compustat tape, proxy statements, and other sources. The final sample for which all the information was available included 228 companies from 28 different industries. Exhibits 8.2 and 8.3 present relevant statistics on ownership structure and performance for the sample firms.

Results

Exhibit 8.4 reports the piecewise linear regression results of profit and market capitalization on ownership structure and diversification strategy.

Exhibit 8.2
Mean Values of Profit and Market Capitalization for 228 *Fortune* 500 Firms in 1987 Grouped by Level of Management Stockholding (MSH)

MSH (%)	Number of firms	Mean profit	Standard error of mean profit	Mean market capitalization	Standard error of mean market capitalization
0–5	154	405.5	879.5	5635.4	8749.2
5–10	29	120.3	133.9	1692.0	1425.9
10–15	16	134.7	167.2	2220.4	2649.6
15–20	7	133.3	91.0	1461.9	773.8
20–25	8	38.3	105.2	1520.0	1215.8
25–30	5	611.7	619.6	8909.8	7904.1
30–35	2	149.0	117.5	2542.3	2246.3
35 40	2	−0.3	70.4	1838.3	255.4
40–45	1	155.2	n/a	2424.5	n/a
45–50	2	154.0	41.5	1745.7	489.9
50–55	0	n/a	n/a	n/a	n/a
55–60	0	n/a	n/a	n/a	n/a
60–65	1	89.6	n/a	1500.3	n/a
65–70	0	n/a	n/a	n/a	n/a
70–75	0	n/a	n/a	n/a	n/a
75–80	0	n/a	n/a	n/a	n/a
80–85	1	186.7	n/a	2443.0	n/a

Source: Belkaoui, Ahmed, and Ellen Pavlik, "The Effect of Ownership Structure and Diversification Strategy in Performance," *Managerial and Decision Economics* 13 (1992): 346. Reprinted with permission.

For comparison purposes the results are presented both with and without the control variable of total assets.

First, as suggested by hypothesis 1, the relationship between performance as measured by profit and market capitalization and management stockholding is negative at a low range of management stockholding (0–5%), positive at a higher range (5–25%), and negative at levels to 25 percent. Basically, for each 1 percent increase in ownership between 0 percent and 5 percent, profit and market capitalization decline, respectively, by an average of 0.0014 and 0.0016. For each 1 percent increase in ownership between 5 percent and 25 percent, profit and market capitalization increase by 0.00029 and 0.0026. As ownership rises beyond 25 percent, both profit and market capitalization decline, respectively, by 0.0000093 and 0.000034.

These results are consistent with both the convergence-of-interests and entrenchment hypotheses. At levels lower than 5 percent, and in accordance with the Berle and Means thesis, the dispersion of shareholders'

Exhibit 8.3
Mean Values of Profit and Market Capitalization for 228 *Fortune* 500 Firms in 1987 Grouped by Level of Stock Concentration (STC)

STC (%)	Number of firms	Mean profit	Standard error of mean profit	Mean market capitalization	Standard error of mean market capitalization
0–5	97	506.7	895.0	6531.9	10164.3
5–10	48	359.3	587.8	4463.6	5550.6
10–15	15	−176.4	1138.3	2474.2	2697.8
15–20	16	143.8	146.7	2012.1	2497.5
20–25	8	112.2	201.9	2008.8	3193.1
25–30	14	110.3	106.0	1539.5	1518.5
30–35	6	107.8	201.5	1102.9	877.4
35–40	6	80.6	131.2	1643.2	1737.3
40–45	3	41.2	88.6	1577.8	589.2
45–50	4	432.2	460.1	7442.7	6098.8
50–55	2	58.0	12.1	1276.6	306.3
55–60	2	151.5	95.8	2106.0	1550.4
60–65	1	8.4	n/a	491.1	n/a
65–70	0	n/a	n/a	n/a	n/a
70–75	0	n/a	n/a	n/a	n/a
75–80	1	157.7	n/a	2689.0	n/a
80–85	3	425.1	566.3	7113.6	5151.3
85–90	2	39.6	20.5	480.2	20.1

Source: Belkaoui, Ahmed, and Ellen Pavlik, "The Effect of Ownership Structure and Diversification Strategy in Performance," *Managerial and Decision Economics* 13 (1992): 347. Reprinted with permission.

ownership allows managers holding little equity to forego value maximization. As managers' stakes in the firm increase beyond 5 percent and in accordance with the convergence-of-interests hypothesis, managers focus more on value maximization. Finally, as their stake in the firm grows very large, beyond 25 percent, and in accordance with the entrenchment hypothesis, managers have enough voting power, tenure, and job guarantee to opt for non-value-maximizing behavior.

Second, as suggested by hypothesis 2, the relationship between stock concentration and performance, as measured by profit and market capitalization, is negative at the low range of stock concentration (0–25%) and positive at the high range of stock concentration (above 25%). Basically, for each 1 percent increase in stock concentration between 0 percent and 5 percent profit and market capitalization decline, respectively, by 0.00083 and 0.00060. As shareholders' ownership rises beyond 5 percent, profit and market capitalization continue to decline, respectively, by 0.00010 and 0.00026. As ownership rises beyond 25 percent, both profit and market capitalization rise, respectively, by 0.00002 and

Exhibit 8.4
Piecewise Linear Ordinary Least-Squares Regression of 1987
Profit and Market Capitalization on Ownership Structure and
Diversification Strategy for 228 *Fortune* 500 Firms[a]

		Dependent variable		
	Profit	Profit	Market capitalization	Market capitalization
Intercept	5.3839	4.8023	8.274	7.7582
Total assets	—	0.00006	—	0.00053
	—	$(0.000005)^b$	—	$(0.0000051)^b$
RTD	0.1445	0.1534	0.1019	0.1104
	$(0.0582)^b$	$(0.0473)^b$	$(0.0499)^c$	$(0.0407)^b$
UTD	0.1843	0.1120	0.1234	0.05749
	$(0.0665)^b$	$(0.0545)^c$	$(0.056)^c$	$(0.0266)^c$
MSH1	−2.8216	−0.1473	−0.2906	−0.1698
	$(0.0504)^b$	$(0.0430)^b$	$(0.0438)^b$	$(0.0375)^b$
MSH2	0.0561	0.0296	0.0475	0.0263
	$(0.0177)^b$	$(0.0146)^c$	$(0.0146)^b$	$(0.0121)^c$
MSH3	−0.0123	−0.00093	−0.00533	−0.00343
	$(0.0050)^b$	$(0.00033)^c$	$(0.0024)^c$	$(0.0019)^d$
STC1	−0.0851	−0.0838	−0.0602	−0.0602
	$(0.0386)^c$	$(0.0314)^b$	$(0.0337)^d$	$(0.02756)^c$
STC2	−0.0237	−0.0107	−0.0365	−0.0265
	$(0.01424)^d$	$(0.004)^b$	$(0.0122)^c$	$(0.01000)^d$
STC3	0.00005	0.00224	0.00798	0.00692
	$(0.00003)^d$	$(0.00134)^d$	$(0.0044)^c$	$(0.0038)^b$
F	9.667^b	24.875^b	13.670^b	30.608^b
R^2	0.2720	0.5208	0.3087	0.5582

[a]Numbers in parentheses are standard errors.
[b]Significant at 99 percent confidence level.
[c]Significant at 95 percent confidence level.
[d]Significant at 90 percent confidence level.

Source: Belkaoui, Ahmed, and Ellen Pavlik, "The Effect of Ownership Structure and Diversification Strategy in Performance," *Managerial and Decision Economics* 13 (1992): 347. Reprinted with permission.

0.000069. These results are consistent with the agency theory view that with a large concentration of stock, stockholders are in a better position to coordinate action, demand information that will allow them to overcome an information asymmetry and influence management's actions toward more value maximization.

Third, as suggested by hypothesis 3, both profit and market capitalization are found to be positively related and unrelated to diversification. The positive relationship is higher with related as opposed to unrelated diversification when assets are used as a control variable. These results show that both profit levels and the market performance of related diversifies are higher than those of the unrelated diversifies.

Fourth, the choice of turning points may be arbitrary. As seen in Exhibit 8.5, various alternative specifications of turning points are chosen. The results conform to those in Exhibit 8.4. Basically,

1. Profit and market capitalization are positively related to related and unrelated diversification, with the impact of related higher than unrelated diversification;
2. Profit and market capitalization are negatively related to ownership structure for low and very high ranges of management stockholding, but positively related to ownership structure for a moderate range of management stockholding; and
3. Profit and market capitalization are negatively related to ownership structure for low to moderate levels of stock concentration and positively related to ownership structure for very high levels of stock concentration.

These results verify the initial results found for the turning point of 5 percent and 25 percent.

Finally, following DL, we estimate a linear relationship between performance, on the one hand, and ownership structure and diversification, on the other. The results using profit and market capitalization as dependent variables are shown in Exhibit 8.6 and reflect a negative relationship between the two types of ownership structure and the two types of performance, as well as a consistently insignificant estimated coefficient on management stockholding, which may be attributed to the failure of a linear specification to capture the important nonmonotonic nature of the relationships.

Conclusion

The results show a significant nonmonotonic relationship between performance and ownership structure and a positive direct relationship between performance and related and unrelated diversification. They indicate that the effects of ownership structure on performance are best examined and explained by taking into account interfirm structural differences.

The significant nonmonotonic relationship between profit and market capitalization, on the one hand, and management stockholding and stock concentration, on the other, is different from the one found by MSV. The results are compatible with a dispersion of ownership and non-value-maximizing behavior by management for less than 5 percent ownership,

Exhibit 8.5
Alternative Piecewise Linear Specification of 1987 Profit and Market Capitalization of Ownership Structure and Diversification (Asset A is a Control Variable)

Panel A: The dependent variable is the 1987 profit

A1: *The turning points are 2.5% and 25% for both MSH_i and STC_i*

$P = 5.15 + 0.00005^a\ A + 0.157^a\ RTD + 0.115^b\ UTD - 0.428^a\ MSH1 + 0.024^b\ MSH2 - 0.00107^c\ MSH3$
$- 0.13^b\ STC1 - 0.014^c\ STC2 + 0.002^c\ STC3$
$F = 26.521,\ R^2 = 0.5368$

A2: *The turning points are 7.5% and 25% for both MSH_i and STC_i*

$P = 4.61 + 0.00005^a\ A + 0.183^a\ RTD + 0.168^a\ UTD - 0.116^a\ MSH1 + 0.049^a\ MSH2 - 0.007^c\ MSH3$
$- 0.08^a\ STC1 - 0.006^c\ STC2 + 0.004^c\ STC3$
$F = 20.815,\ R^2 = 0.5425$

A3: *The turning points are 5% and 15% for both MSH_i and STC_i*

$P = 4.80 + 0.00006^a\ A + 0.149^a\ RTD + 0.114^b\ UTD - 0.14^a\ MSH1 + 0.077^c\ MSH2 - 0.0061^c\ MSH3$
$- 0.069^b\ STC1 - 0.029^c\ STC2 + 0.0011^c\ STC3$
$F = 24.92,\ R^2 = 0.5213$

A4: *The turning points are 5% and 20% for both MSH_i and STC_i*

$P = 4.80 + 0.00006^a\ A + 0.151^a\ RTD + 0.112^b\ UTD - 0.145^a\ MSH1 + 0.031^c\ MSH2 - 0.003^c\ MSH3$
$- 0.078^b\ STC1 - 0.016^c\ STC2 + 0.0015^c\ STC3$
$F = 24.831,\ R^2 = 0.5203$

A5: *The turning points are 5% and 30% for both MSH_i and STC_i*

$P = 4.79 + 0.00006^a\ A + 0.154^a\ RTD + 0.111^b\ UTD - 0.145^a\ MSH1 + 0.026^b\ MSH2 - 0.003^c\ MSH3$
$- 0.08^a\ STC1 - 0.008^c\ STC2 + 0.0026^c\ STC3$
$F = 24.853,\ R = 0.5206$

Panel B: The dependent variable is the 1987 market capitalization

B1: *The turning points are 2.5% and 25% for both MSH_i and STC_i*

$MC = 8.06 + 0.00005^a\ A + 0.115^a\ RTD + 0.059^c\ UTD - 0.42^a\ MSH1 + 0.01^c\ MSH2 - 0.006^c\ MSH3$
$- 0.075^c\ STC1 - 0.030^a\ STC2 + 0.005^c\ STC3$
$F = 31.77,\ R^2 = 0.5674$

B2: *The turning points are 7.5% and 25% for both MSH_i and STC_i*

$MC = 7.56 + 0.00005^a\ A + 0.129^a\ RTD + 0.116^b\ UTD - 0.119^a\ MSH1 + 0.039^b\ MSH2 - 0.001^c\ MSH3$
$- 0.063^a\ STC1 - 0.021^c\ STC2 + 0.011^c\ STC3$
$F = 24.495,\ R^2 = 0.5645$

B3: *The turning points are 5% and 15% for both MSH_i and STC_i*

$MC = 7.74 + 0.00005^a\ A + 0.11^a\ RTD + 0.06^c\ UTD - 0.16^a\ MSH1 + 0.028^c\ MSH2 - 0.009^c\ MSH3$
$- 0.005^c\ STC1 - 0.046^b\ STC2 + 0.002^c\ STC3$

Exhibit 8.5 (Continued)

$F = 30.182, R^2 = 0.5548$

B4: *The turning points are 5% and 20% for both MSH_i and STC_i*

$MC = 7.74 + 0.00005^a\ A + 0.11^a\ RTD + 0.059^c\ UTD - 0.166^a\ MSH1 + 0.025^c\ MSH2 - 0.007^c\ MSH3$
$- 0.056^b\ STC1 - 0.033^a\ STC2 + 0.004^c\ STC3$

$F = 30.33, R^2 = 0.5560$

B5: *The turning points are 5% and 30% for both MSH_i and STC_i*

$MC = 7.76 + 0.00005^a\ A + 0.11^a\ RTD + 0.054^b\ UTD - 0.173^a\ MSH1 + 0.02^a\ MSH2 - 0.001^c\ MSH3$
$- 0.06^b\ STC1 - 0.022^a\ STC2 + 0.009^c\ STC3$

$F = 30.932, R^2 = 0.5608$

[a]Significant at 99 percent confidence level.
[b]Significant at 95 percent confidence level.
[c]Significant at 90 percent confidence level.

Source: Belkaoui, Ahmed, and Ellen Pavlik, "The Effect of Ownership Structure and Diversification Strategy in Performance," *Managerial and Decision Economics* 13 (1992): 348. Reprinted with permission.

a convergence of interests between managers and shareholders between 5 percent and 25 percent ownership, and an entrenchment of the management team as their stakes exceed 25 percent. Similarly, the results suggest the need for large stock concentration before shareholders can influence management decisions toward value-maximizing behavior.

The results on the impact of management stockholding and the stock concentration on performance are compatible with a model that views the interests of shareholders and managers as fundamentally in conflict over the issue of risk.[20] Managers may be wedded to their jobs, whereas shareholders have diversified their portfolios. Therefore, the managers will act in a more risk-averse manner than the shareholders and will be protective of their autonomy. The results show that this "risk-aversion differential" between managers and shareholders and the resulting "excess earnings retention" are more compatible with high rather than low management stockholding and stock concentration. The higher level of management stockholding allowed the kind of retrenchment and organizational slack on which earlier generations of managerial critics have focused.[21] Takeover is the means by which the market may purge the modern corporation of this organizational slack. The results indicate that the turning of the takeover is more likely with higher than lower levels of management stockholding and stock concentration.

Exhibit 8.6
Simple Linear Regression of 1987 Profit and Market Capitalization on Ownership Structure and Diversification Strategy for 228 *Fortune* 500 Firms[a]

	Profit	Profit	Market capitalization	Market capitalization
			Dependent variable	
Intercept	4.631	4.335	7.470	7.196
Total assets	—	0.000068	—	0.00006
	—	(0.0000058)[b]	—	(0.000005)[b]
RTD	0.1531	0.1521	0.1212	0.1201
	(0.0629)[b]	(0.048)[b]	(0.0562)[c]	(0.0438)
UTD	0.1802	0.053	0.1226	0.0399
	(0.0720)[b]	(0.056)[c]	(0.0637)[c]	(0.0503)
MSH	−0.008	−0.0015	−0.0118	−0.0049
	(0.007)	(0.0057)	(0.0065)	(0.005)
STC	−0.0172	−0.0124	−0.0153	−0.011
	(0.0044)[b]	(0.0034)[b]	(0.0038)[b]	(0.0030)[b]
F	6.917[b]	36.815[b]	7.483[b]	38.520
R²	0.1159	0.4671	0.1183	0.4645

[a]Numbers in parentheses are standard errors computed according to White (1980).
[b]Significant at 99 percent confidence level.
[c]Significant at 95 percent confidence level.

Source: Belkaoui, Ahmed, and Ellen Pavlik, "The Effect of Ownership Structure and Diversification Strategy in Performance," *Managerial and Decision Economics* 13 (1992): 350. Reprinted with permission.

THE EFFECTS OF OWNERSHIP STRUCTURE ON VALUE ADDED–BASED PERFORMANCE

This chapter argues that the effects of ownership structure on performance are best examined when performance expresses total return rather than being restricted to accounting return. More explicitly, the study develops and tests a model that describes the influence of ownership structure on a value added–based measure of performance.

Ownership Structure and Value Added–Based Performance

Because value added is a measure of the total performance of a firm, both shareholders and managers would be interested in its value, but for different reasons. First, given low stock concentration and low management stockholding, the dispersion of shareholders' ownership allows managers who themselves hold little equity in the firm to forego total return maximization as measured by net value added. The expectation is that the rate of return on assets, when return is measured by net value added, will decline with low stock concentration and low management stockholding.

Second, given high stock concentration and high management stockholding, managers, both at the urging of stockholders and on their own, are motivated to increase the total return of the firm as measured by the net value added, in accordance with a convergence-of-interests hypothesis. The expectations of managers and shareholders are, however, different. Managers holding a high stake in the firm and having substantial voting power, tenure, and job security are interested in a higher net value in order to guarantee them higher perquisites in the form of higher compensation and benefits, at the expense of a lower accounting profit. Shareholders are interested in a higher net value added with the expectation of a higher distribution of profits.

In short, performance as measured by a rate of return based on net value added will decline for lower ranges of share ownership by either managers or shareholders, and will increase for higher ranges of share ownership by either managers or shareholders. Accordingly, the following three hypothesis will be tested:

H_1: There will be a negative relationship between a firm's performance based on net value added and stock concentration at a lower range, and a positive relationship between the same performance measure and stock concentration at a higher range.

H_2: There will be a negative relationship between a firm's performance based on net value added and management stockholding at a lower range, and a positive relationship between the same performance measure and management stockholding at a higher range.

H_3: There will be a negative relationship between a firm's performance based on net value added and the sum of stock concentration and management stockholding at a lower range, and a positive relationship between the same performance measure and the sum of stock concentration and management stockholding at a higher range.

The piecewise linear regression models allowing for one change in the slope coefficient for the measures of ownership structure are used. The first stage of this analysis utilizes a turning point of 10 percent. Later stages of the analysis will test the sensitivity to alternative specification of the turning point.

Methods

Dependent Variable

The net value numerator was computed as follows: net value added (NVA) = the sum of labor expenses, corporate taxes, interest expenses, and minority shareholders in subsidiaries plus retained earnings. The dependent variable expressing a total rate of return of a firm was chosen as the net value added dividend by the total assets of the firm.

Ownership Structure

This study avoided the weaknesses of studies that relied on a single dichotomous variable contrasting owner and management control, defined on the basis of some arbitrary statistical criterion for size of controlling interest. It also did not rely on the 1980 data assembled one time only by Corporate Data Exchange and utilized by most contemporary studies on ownership structure. Instead, the data were collected from the 1988 proxy statement information for the individual firms. The stock concentration measured was computed as the percentage ownership by outside stockholders owning more than 5 percent of the common voting stock in 1988. Management stockholding was measured by the percentage of common voting stock held by management (officers and directors) in 1988.

Sample

To ensure the greatest sample of firms for which data would be available for ownership structure and value added–based measures of performance, the initial sample chosen was the total number of firms in Compustat disclosing all the information needed for the computation of net value added. The next step involved the collection of the needed information on assets and ownership structure from the Compustat tape and the proxy statements. The final sample for which all the information

Exhibit 8.7
Mean Values of Net Value Added over Total Assets for 394 Firms in 1988 Grouped by Level of Management Stockholding (MSH)

MSH	Number of Firms	Mean Net Value Added Over Total Assets	Standard Error Net Value Added Over Total Assets
0- 5%	232	0.2233	0.1633
5-10%	44	0.1800	0.1753
10-15%	31	0.1670	0.1591
15-20%	12	0.2254	0.2195
20-25%	19	0.2023	0.1529
25-30%	8	0.3330	0.1927
30-35%	9	0.1763	0.1562
35-40%	10	0.2321	0.1687
40-45%	7	0.3807	0.2560
45-50%	3	0.1526	0.0740
50-55%	4	0.2358	0.1181
55-60%	3	0.4033	0.1600
60-65%	2	0.0523	0.0180
65-70%	5	0.2962	0.2418
70-75%	1	0.2975	n/a
75-80%	1	0.0459	n/a
80-85%	0	n/a	n/a
85-90%	3	0.4281	0.1120

Source: Riahi-Belkaoui, Ahmed, and Ellen Pavlik, ''The Effect of Ownership Structure on Value Added-Based Performance,'' *Managerial Finance* 20, no. 9 (1994): 20. Reprinted with permission.

was available included 394 companies representing 32 different industries.

Exhibits 8.7 and 8.8 present relevant statistics on ownership structure and net value added over total assets for the firms included in the sample.

Results

The following various results emerge: First, Exhibit 8.9 reports the piecewise linear regression results of net value added over assets on

Exhibit 8.8
Mean Values of Net Value Added over Total Assets for 394 Firms in 1988 Grouped by Level of Stock Concentration (STC)

STC	Number of Firms	Mean Net Value Added Over Total Assets	Standard Error Net Value Added Over Total Assets
0- 5%	156	0.2331	0.1643
5-10%	66	0.2015	0.1706
10-15%	36	0.2211	0.1786
15-20%	32	0.1954	0.1591
20-25%	23	0.1902	0.1834
25-30%	18	0.1511	0.1409
30-35%	15	0.2303	0.2050
35-40%	6	0.1669	0.1759
40-45%	10	0.1569	0.1356
45-50%	6	0.2973	0.1579
50-55%	5	0.4497	0.1193
55-60%	4	0.2739	0.1425
60-65%	4	0.3353	0.2431
65-70%	5	0.2182	0.2093
70-75%	3	0.2716	0.2491
75-80%	1	0.6508	n/a
80-85%	1	0.1696	n/a
85-90%	0	n/a	n/a
90-95%	3	0.1621	0.1185

Source: Riahi-Belkaoui, Ahmed, and Ellen Pavlik, "The Effect of Ownership Structure on Value Added-Based Performance," *Managerial Finance* 20, no. 9 (1994): 21. Reprinted with permission.

ownership structure. As suggested by hypotheses 1, 2, and 3, the relationship between net value added over assets and measures of ownership structure, management stockholding, and stock concentration, separately or summed, is negative at a low range of ownership structure (0 to 10%) and positive at a higher level (greater than 10%). Basically, at levels lower than 10 percent, the dispersion of shareholders' ownership allows managers holding themselves little equity to forego total return maximization as measured by net value added. As managers' and sharehold-

Exhibit 8.9
**Piecewise Linear Ordinary Least-Squares Regression for Net
Value Added over Total Assets on Ownership Structure for 394
Firms Using a Turning Point of 10 Percent**

Independent Variables	Model 1	Model 2
Intercept	0.2347 (15.211)*	0.2604 (14.476)*
MSH[1], 0 to 10%	−0.0046 (−1.687)***	————
MSH, 10% to 100%	0.1122 (2.854)*	————
SC[2], 0–10%	−0.0032 (−1.526)***	————
SC, 10%–100%	0.0012 (1.833)***	————
TOS[3], 0–10%	————	−0.0098 (−3.792)*
TOS, 10%–100%	————	0.0017 (3.831)*
R^2	0.0309	0.0460
F	3.112**	9.446*

[1] MSH = management stockholdings.
[2] SC = stock concentration.
[3] TOS = MSH + SC.
  *Significant at $\alpha = 0.01$.
 **Significant at $\alpha = 0.05$.
***Significant at $\alpha = 0.10$.

Source: Riahi-Belkaoui, Ahmed, and Ellen Pavlik, "The Effect of Ownership Structure on Value
    Added-Based Performance," *Managerial Finance* 20, no. 9 (1994): 22. Reprinted with per-
    mission.

ers' stakes in the firm increase beyond 10 percent, the managers start
focusing more on generating a higher value added as they find their
interest in the firm converging with the shareholders', in accordance with
the convergence-of-interest hypothesis.

This result is not in contradiction with other studies' results where in
accordance with the entrenchment hypothesis, managers holding a high
stake in the firm have enough voting power, tenure, and job guarantee

to opt for non-value-maximizing behaviors as based on a profit-based measure of performance. The results of this study show that managers favor an increase in the total returns as measured by net value added that would guarantee higher perquisites in the form of higher compensation and benefits and that would decrease the profit level of the firm. In brief, at higher levels of ownership, managers and shareholders prefer a higher net value added for different reasons. Managers prefer this outcome for higher compensation and benefits. Shareholders prefer the same outcome with the expectation of higher profit distribution.

Second, as suggested earlier, the choice of the turning point may be arbitrary. As seen in Exhibit 8.10, various alternative specifications of turning points have been chosen. The results conform to the previously reported results in Exhibit 8.9 up to the turning point of 25 percent. Basically, net value added over total assets, as a measure of a total rate of return, is negatively related to the three measures of ownership structure at lower levels and positively related to the same measures at higher levels. The three measures of ownership structure are management stockholding, stock concentration, and the sum of management stockholding and stock concentration.

CONCLUSIONS

In this section the effects of ownership structure on total performance of the firm as measured by value added–based performance were examined. A differentiation is made between management stockholding and stock concentration. The results show a significant nonmonotonic relationship between value added–based performance and ownership structure. Whether ownership structure is measured by management stockholding, stock concentration, or the sum of the two measures, value added–based performance declines up to a turning point before the increasing proportionally to the increases in ownership structure measures. The interpretation is compatible with (a) a dispersion of ownership and non-value-maximizing behavior holding less than 10 percent ownership and (b) a convergence of interests for the maximization of value added–based performance between managers and shareholders for more than 10 percent ownership.

One important policy implication of this study is the need to focus on value added–based performance rather than profit-based performance to better understand the diverse interests of shareholders and managers. Thus an important accounting policy issue is whether U.S. firms should

Exhibit 8.10
Piecewise Linear Ordinary Least-Squares Regression for Net Value Added over Total Assets on Ownership Structure for 394 Firms

Variables	x = 5%		x = 7%		x = 15%		x = 20%		x = 25%	
	Model 1	Model 2	Model 1	Model 2	Model 1	Model 2	Model 1	Model 2	Model 1	Model 2
Intercept	0.2450* (14.510)	0.2631 (12.82)	0.2405* (14.878)	0.2615* (13.581)	0.2307* (15.697)	0.2580 (15.535)	0.2269 (15.953)	0.2527 (16.072)	0.2250 (16.208)	0.2483 (16.493)
MSH, 0 - x%	-0.0118** (-2.343)	—	-0.0079** (-2.107)	—	-0.0021 (-1.107)	—	-0.0008 (-0.600)	—	-0.0002 (-0.181)	—
MSH, x - 100%	0.0020* (3.080)	—	0.0021* (3.040)	—	0.0022** (2.507)	—	0.0021** (2.155)	—	0.0020** (1.848)	—
SC, 0 - x%	-0.0062 (-1.456)	—	-0.0045 (-1.445)	—	-0.0026*** (-1.631)	—	-0.0021 (-1.656)	—	-0.0018* (-1.775)	—
SC, x - 100%	0.0010*** (1.705)	—	0.0011*** (1.774)	—	0.0015** (2.067)	—	0.0017* (2.187)	—	0.0021* (2.411)	—
TOS, 0 - x%	—	-0.0180* (-3.317)	—	-0.1324* (-3.516)	—	-0.0068* (-4.070)	—	-0.0049* (-3.938)	—	-0.0037* (-3.762)
TOS, x - 100%	—	0.0013* (3.228)	—	0.0014* (3.470)	—	0.0021* (4.322)	—	0.0023* (4.505)	—	0.0026 (4.636)
R^2	0.0354	0.0352	0.0342	0.0394	0.0298	0.0547	0.0275	0.0559	0.0276	0.0567
F	3.574*	7.141*	3.450*	8.039*	2.998**	11.352*	2.760**	11.597*	2.769**	11.774*

*Significant at $\alpha = 0.01$.
**Significant at $\alpha = 0.05$.
***Significant at $\alpha = 0.10$.

Source: Riahi-Belkaoui, Ahmed, and Ellen Pavlik, "The Effect of Ownership Structure on Value Added-Based Performance," *Managerial Finance* 20, no. 9 (1994): 23. Reprinted with permission.

be required to disclose the underlying data needed to compute the value added. At present, less than 10 percent of the firms listed on Compustat consistently disclose labor expenses, a key variable. The cost of reporting this data may be immaterial as firms process this information for payroll purposes and report this to the government. It can be easily concluded that value added reporting is very useful and ought to be disclosed by U.S. firms.

NOTES

1. Monsen, R. J., and A. Downs, "A Theory of Large Managerial Firms," *Journal of Political Economy* 73 (1965): 65–75.

2. Williamson, O. E., *The Economics of Discretionary Behavior: Managerial Objective in a Theory of the Firm* (Englewood Cliffs, NJ: Prentice-Hall, 1964).

3. Demsetz, H., "The Structure of Ownership and the Theory of the Firm," *Journal of Law and Economics* 26 (1983): 375–390.

4. Cubbin, J., and D. Leech, "The Effect of Shareholder Dispersion on the Degree of Control in British Companies: Theory and Measurement," *Economic Journal* 93 (1983): 351–369.

5. Ibid.

6. Hill, C. W., and S. A. Snell, "Effects of Ownership Structure and Control on Corporate Productivity," *Academy of Management Journal* 32 (1989): 25–46.

7. Morck, R. A., A. Schleifer, and R. W. Vishny, "Management Ownership and Market Valuation: An Empirical Analysis," *Journal of Financial Economics* 20 (1988): 293–315.

8. Demsetz, H., and K. Lehn, "The Structure of Corporate Ownership: Theory and Consequences," *Journal of Political Economy* 93 (1985): 1155–1177.

9. Riahi-Belkaoui, Ahmed, *The New Foundation of Management Accounting* (Westport, CT: Greenwood Publishing Co. 1992).

10. Berle, A. A., and G. C. Means, *The Modern Corporation* (New York: Macmillan, 1932).

11. Manne, H. "Mergers and the Market for Corporate Control," *Journal of Political Economy* 73 (1965): 110–120.

12. Fama, E. F., "Agency Problems and the Theory of the Firms," *Journal of Political Economy* 88 (1980): 288–307.

13. Shavell, S., "Risk Sharing and Incentives in the Principal and Agent Relationship," *Bell Journal of Economics* 10 (1979): 55–73.

14. Jensen, M., "Agency Costs of Fair Cash Flow Corporate Finance and Takeover," *The American Economic Review* 26 (1986): 323–399.

15. Jensen, M., and W. H. Meckling, "Theory of the Firm and Managerial

Behavior, Agency Costs, and Ownership Structure," *Journal of Finance* 3 (1976): 305–360.

16. Ibid.

17. Hart, O. D. "The Market Mechanism as an Incentive Scheme," *Rell Journal of Economics* 14 (1983): 366–382.

18. Jensen, M., and R. Ruback, "The Market for Corporate Control: The Scientific Evidence," *Journal of Financial Economics* 11 (1983): 5–50.

19. Morris, R., *The Economic Theory of Managerial Capitalism* (London: Macmillan, 1964).

20. Coffee, J. C., "Shareholders Versus Managers: The Strain in the Corporate Web," *Knights, Raiders, and Targets: The Impact of the Hostile Takeover,* ed. J. C. Coffee et al. (Oxford: Oxford University Press, 1988).

21. Ibid.

REFERENCES

Barrett, M. J., W. H. Beaver, W. W. Cooper, J. A. Milburn, D. Solomon, and D. P. Tweedie. "Report of the American Accounting Association Committee on Accounting and Auditing Measurement, 1989–1990." *Accounting Horizon* (September 1991): 81–105.

Belkaoui, A. *Value Added Reporting: The Lessons for the U.S.* Westport, CT: Quorum Books, 1992.

Berle, A. A., and G. C. Means. *The Modern Corporation.* New York: Macmillan, 1932.

Cubbin, J., and D. Leech. "The Effect of Shareholder Dispersion on the Degree of Control in British Companies: Theory and Measurement." *Economic Journal* 93 (1983): 351–369.

Demsetz, H., and K. Lehn. "The Structure of Corporate Ownership: Theory and Consequences." *Journal of Political Economy* 93 (1985): 1155–1177.

Gray, S. J., and K. T. Maunders. *Value Added Reporting: Uses and Measurement.* London: Association of Certified Accountants, 1988.

Hermalin, B. E., and M. S. Weisbad. "The Effects of Board Composition on Corporate Performance." Working Paper, Massachusetts Institute of Technology, 1987.

Hill, C. W., and S. A. Snell. "Effects of Ownership Structure and Control on Corporate Productivity" *Academy of Management Journal* 32 (1989): 25–46.

Holderness, C. G., and D. P. Sheehan. "Raiders or Saviors? The Evidence on Six Controversial Investors." *Journal of Financial Economics* 14 (1985): 555–579.

Jensen, M., and W. H. Meckling. "Theory of the Firm and Managerial Behavior, Agency Costs, and Ownership Structure." *Journal of Financial Economics* 3 (1976): 305–360.

Karpik, P., and A. Belkaoui. "The Relative Relationship between Systematic Risk and Value Added Variables." *Journal of International Financial Management and Accounting* (Spring 1989): 259–276.

Meek, G. K., and S. J. Gray. "The Value Added Statement: Innovation for U.S. Companies." *Accounting Horizons* (June 1988): 73–81.

Morck, R. A., A. Shleifer, and R. W. Vishny. "Management Ownership and Market Valuation: An Empirical Analysis." *Journal of Financial Economics* 20 (1988): 293–315.

Riahi-Belkaoui, A., and E. Pavlik. "The Effect of Ownership Structure and Diversification Strategy in Performance." *Managerial and Decision Economics* 13 (1992) 343–352.

Stulz, R. "Managerial Control of Voting Rights, Financial Policies and the Market for Corporate Control." *Journal of Financial Economics* 20 (1988): 25–54.

Index

About the Author

AHMED RIAHI-BELKAOUI is Professor of Accounting in the College of Business Administration, University of Illinois at Chicago. A prolific author of journal articles and scholarly and professional books and textbooks, he serves on the editorial boards of numerous prestigious journals in his field and is known for his unusual, often groundbreaking research and analysis. This is his twenty-eighth Quorum book.

ISBN 1-56720-024-9

EAN

9 781567 200249

HARDCOVER BAR CODE